Empowering

Dyslexics

Blessed and Gifted

Keisha Adair Swaby

Empowering Dyslexics

Blessed and Gifted

Authored by Keisha Adair Swaby

Foreword by Marcia Brissett-Bailey

ISBN: 978-1-913905-73-6

MARCIA M
PUBLISHING HOUSE

www.marciampublishing.com

Dedications

I have to start by thanking God for taking me this far on my journey after all the challenges I have encountered. Secondly, my parents, thank you for all you have done for me. Daddy, I know how proud you will be to know your daughter has written her first book and is now an author. Thank you for the sacrifices you made when I was growing up to make sure I went to school. Growing up with you was amazing, and I will be forever grateful for the love you showed and how you cared for me. My mom and grandmas, I know how strong you all are, and I know that having your genes has shaped me into the woman I am today. A massive thank you to all the strong women in my family.

I have so many people to thank for my journey. The support from my amazing family has been on another level.

Firstly, my husband – you have been my rock since we met. You have supported me with all the crazy, wonderful ideas I have had over the years. Without your support, I couldn't have achieved half the things I have. You know me, and you know how much I love helping people. You have never questioned what I do. Even when I flew all the way to Jamaica to do my voluntary work with *Jamaicans Inspired*, you held everything down like a true boss. I appreciate you and all you do for our family. Being dyslexic isn't easy, and you have helped me so much even with the little things that you do, like directing me in the car, so I don't go around the roundabout a hundred times; you have been my satnav on so many journeys. You do little things like making sure my telephone is fully charged when I am going out on my own so that I can use the satnav on my telephone to get me where I need to be. Every year when the clocks change, you always make sure you set the clock five minutes fast so I am not as late as I could be. It's the little things you do to make things easier for me.

My beautiful children: Dellea, Aljay, Alexa and Aaron. I'm so glad that you two are twin boys and girls, as I am sure I wouldn't know which is which (other dyslexics will get it).

Dellea, I want to give appreciation for all you do for your family and friends. I am so proud of the beautiful young lady you have become, and I want you to always shine your light for your siblings, as you are the best role model they could ask for. You are so independent and driven. It has been a delight watching your journey. I was so proud when we both graduated a week apart.

Seeing you walking across that stage on your graduation day after you achieved a first-class honours degree in international business and marketing was one of my proudest moments. You are truly the queen of my heart.

Special
Dedication

Special dedication to my Aunt Vilma, who Passed away on the 26th of July 2021

My dear auntie, I wish you were here to see me become an author. I thank you for all you have done for your family and me, near and far. You inspired me to be strong and never to give up. Even in your struggles and challenges, you never gave up, and even in your time of sickness, you still never gave up. You were given six to eight weeks to live but lived way beyond that. You will always be missed, and I promise to continue on my own journey to being strong and determined, just like you. Thank you for being the auntie you were. I promise to continue to make you proud. Rest in peace. You are loved and remembered.

A note to
my children:

You are all so unique in your own special way. Aljay you are so clever with numbers you impress me so much because you truly have a skill that you should lead with in your future. Continue to be the bright and loving Son that you are. I love how you are protective of your siblings. Your love for football is simply great to see. As you grow and mature remember to strive to be all that you dream of and don't be held back in chasing all the dreams and goals that has been placed in your heart. I love you Son and continue to make us proud each and every day. (JJ Roo)

Alexa my young Queen, I want you to believe in yourself and continue with your creativity and your love of art and making things. Thanks for always offering a helping hand in the kitchen and around the house. Your love for your siblings pour out each day as you are always there looking out for them each day. You have your own challenges being diagnosed with Dyspraxia but don't ever think it can stop you from doing all the great things that you are good at and meant to do. I love you dearly and I cherish our bond. Go out three and shine my little Queen.

Aaron my cheeky boy with so much confidence, you are definitely the joker in our family with your amazing sense of humour and liveliness around the house. There is never a dull moment with you around. Thank you for the joy you bring to us all. I can see a very bright future for you as an entrepreneur or an entertainer as you have so many creative ideas and the confidence to speak to anyone. You are absolutely amazing, and your cuteness existed from the day you were born as you were the twin that I nearly lost when I was giving birth to you both. You was the happiest baby I have ever seen, and you have continued with that joy happiness all the way.

I thank you all for your love, support and patience especially whilst I was writing this book. As you all go through life be reminded that you can be anything you want to be, and you can achieve whatever you put your mind to. I love you all more than you will ever know. Always remember your daily I AMs that I have taught you all! I AM amazing, I AM powerful, I CAN do anything, I CAN achieve anything!

Foreword

When you find a sister in someone who is not blood, you keep them close. Keisha Adair Swaby, AKA Lady K, is that someone. She is my Dyslexic soul sister.

When we get together, Keisha and I can speak for England, but ironically, we both selectively muted at school within the British education system. Just through traumatic experiences for Keisha, she was bullied at school for her Jamaican accent; this really resonates with me. I did not want to read aloud, so I decided to selectively mute too in order to make myself invisible; there are so many intersectional layers that can knock a person's confidence and self-esteem when you are told you're not good enough.

We are both of Jamaican heritage and from the parish of Saint Elizabeth. From our conversations, we discovered that we both grew up with aunties and grandparents. Which provided aspects of our roots and culture, in which we learnt the old-school values of having good manners. We were always told that good manners can take you a long way. Culture can really provide identity and a sense of belonging and define how we show up in the world in terms of our identity.

I never need to explain my experience of exclusion, feeling different, isolation, representation, culture or a lack of belonging. The missing gaps, leaving school with no GCSE's is a story we both know well and a commonality between us, which is a significant part of Keisha's journey.

Her story is very much entwined with early childhood trauma, community trauma, generational trauma and collective trauma, from not feeling good enough or having safe spaces to find her voice. Societal infrastructures where not kind and systematic barriers are very real and go far beyond representation.

This book highlights the need to have a strong belief in your abilities and the courage to pursue your dreams, whatever they may be, without fearing failure.

Despite the challenges that Keisha encountered, she has proved that there is hope through her resilience, hunger for empowerment, and determination to achieve her dreams and goals.

Keisha's story also tells us about never giving up. It shows us the power of taking that leap of faith to achieve her goals.

She visualised her dream of wearing her cap and gown at graduation. It was at university Keisha was diagnosed with Dyslexia and Dyspraxia, and everything became clearer about some of the challenges she had experienced in education and the workplace.

I hope you will read this book and feel inspired with a realisation that anything is possible, as well as opening up a deeper conversation about diversity and inclusion alongside neurodiversity and its impact from an intersectional lens. It is very timely as, for far too long, we have not heard the voices of neurodiverse Black people, and Keisha is part of that change for today, but also for tomorrow in inspiring others to find their own voice.

It's time for organisations and educational institutions to create initiatives that will allow neurodiversity and inclusivity, alongside feeling emotionally safe with reasonable adjustments and support to thrive.

I wish I was told at school to embrace my differences and know that no one is perfect and that we can all have a sense of belonging in Keisha's words:

> *"No one is born perfect. Don't be afraid. People can accomplish amazing things every day in spite of their weaknesses and challenges. So go and do the best you can with the one life you've got."*

Marcia Brissett-Bailey, AKA *theblackdyslexic*, named one of the **Top 50 Influential Neurodivergent Women 2022, BDA Adult Award 2022, and** *Top 80 Neurodiversity Evangelist UK 2023*, editor of the book Black, Brilliant and Dyslexic.

Empowering

Dyslexics

Blessed and Gifted

Keisha Adair Swaby

Contents

Why have I
written this book?

I have always loved writing, and while I left school with no GCSEs, I have a passion for writing and a dream to make a difference in this world. The main reason for writing this book is to create more awareness with the hope of helping others to understand more about dyslexia and dyspraxia by highlighting the brilliance of our superpowers.

Others won't know your story until you tell it! We can truly inspire and empower others through the sharing of our stories. When I was younger, I was ashamed of my story, but I learnt that I shouldn't be. Your story can help others who might be going through the same thing.

Many have dyslexia, and many don't know they have it! It took me an exceptionally long time to finally get to the bottom of things, and now it's my time to share my story so that it can help others and prevent them from going through what I have. Trust me, it hasn't been an easy journey, and I really don't want anyone to go through it.

It has been said that one in five people have dyslexia or another learning difference. I choose to call these traits learning differences, as that's what they are. However, everyone who is neurodiverse has their own strengths and challenges. I truly believe that more than one in five people have dyslexia. My reason for saying so is that I have a group of seven speakers, and three of us are diagnosed with dyslexia and dyspraxia, while the other four haven't been assessed. I have been in a room with two other people, and all three of us were dyslexic. This is why I have a strong belief that statistics do not reflect reality. The number of dyslexic people could be significantly more because people are unaware, they have these learning differences as they have never been assessed.

Having these learning differences doesn't mean there is anything wrong with you, just that we understand and interpret things differently. It can often become a battle trying to explain to others if they don't understand how people are affected and how they can be supported.

A lot of my determination to write this book has been inspired by my own children, to help them and generations to come. After my own diagnosis at the age of 41 and after my daughter Dellea was also diagnosed, I came to realise the challenges she had in school were due to her undiagnosed dyspraxia. I remember when she was in primary school, she really struggled, and I wasn't able to support her because I was having my own challenges, which I didn't understand at the time due to my own undiagnosed learning differences. At that time, I didn't know how to get or give her the support she needed. At times I felt I had let her down and wished I knew I had dyslexia while she was at school to give her the support she needed in her early years.

Some may be thinking, so what? A lot of people have dyslexia and other learning differences, so what makes me an expert? My answer is simple: I have lived with it all my life, and it has affected me in more ways than you could imagine! However, I have learnt to embrace my strengths and now recognise why I enjoy doing certain tasks while also having struggles with other things. With all the challenges I faced, I didn't let dyslexia and dyspraxia hinder me from achieving my dreams and goals. Throughout my life, I have developed my own way of doing things, and finding solutions and seeing the bigger picture is a great dyslexic strength. Our brains are dynamic;

dyslexics have the ability to think in more ways than one.

People with dyslexia possess amazing strengths, and because of their challenges, they develop their own ways of overcoming these. It can be easy for people with dyslexia to mask what they are going through because they do things very well and are highly skilled, so most people around them, like family members and friends, are not aware of their daily struggles. There is still a lot of stigma, embarrassment and shame surrounding these learning differences, and my mission is to create more awareness, empower others and help them to realise they are gifted and possess many amazing strengths.

Who is this book for?

I wrote this book for anyone who wants to know more about these learning differences. For anyone who feels they do things 'differently' to other people.

It's for the parent that wants to know what to look out for in their own children. This book is a useful tool for understanding more about my own story and my lived experience. It's to help discover why dyslexics falter when doing certain things. It's for the girl who is confused as to why she feels clumsy all the time, for the boy who feels frustrated and stupid in front of his friends for not being able to take simple instructions or always getting lost on journeys. It is for anyone who feels they cannot own up to having something the majority of society never experience. It's for that woman who often leaves her bank card in the machine or loses her purse (yep, it all happened to me). It's for all the children who slipped through the net and didn't get diagnosed when they were in school. It's for everyone who took the plunge and went on to higher education, finally getting the diagnosis that changed their world for the better and helped them to get the support they needed.

It's for the woman who didn't get that promotion because her challenges with maths meant she couldn't pass the test.

It's for teachers who don't know about dyslexia and dyspraxia and how they can support their pupils. It's for all the people in our communities who often wonder why they struggle to read, write or spell. It's for all the people who feel ashamed or that they cannot come to terms with there being something amiss, but they feel if they own up to having a learning difference, people will see them differently and think less of them.

Why suffer in silence? I did for many years (41 years, actually), and I don't want others to continue just getting through life when they feel they could achieve more. So many people have wondered whether they are 'stupid' or 'thick' and have been called these names growing up and still hear them today. I used to question my own abilities from the limitations placed on me by others. So many dots will be connected when you finally know why you do things the way you do. It will be a life-changing experience to finally get the confidence to be who you actually are and can be with the right support. You can be someone who is truly blessed!

I am sharing my own lived experience with the hope of helping someone realise they are not 'daft,' 'slow' or 'stupid'. No, far from it: we just learn and do things differently and can be highly intelligent. People are not those definitions and names we are labelled with, and that negative name-calling has affected many, including me.

Several well-known dyslexics have great abilities, such as Sir Steve McQueen, who is an amazing writer with many accolades for his contribution to the arts and media, and the great poet Benjamin Zephaniah. Maggie Aderin-Pocock is an amazing dyslexic scientist who prides herself in not just thinking outside the box but the whole planet. I love her emphasis on seeing dyslexia as a learning difference rather than a disability, something which everyone should understand and see the positives, as every child has their own unique strengths. Other talented dyslexics include Will Smith, Whoopi Goldberg, Walt Disney, Steven Spielberg, Albert Einstein, Sir Richard Branson, plus many more. I have always admired these amazing people, their business spirit, and all that they have achieved. It feels like an honour to be dyslexic like them. Oh yes, dyslexic people can be very entrepreneurial because they have the ability to think outside of the box without limitations.

Another example of dyslexic greatness is Erna Solberg, the former Prime Minister of Norway. She is another proud dyslexic who has said: "I myself cannot spell, have never been able to. I do not pay attention to spelling and mix letters."

What is dyslexia?

"If you are dyslexic and you feel there's something holding you back, just remember it's not you. In many ways being dyslexic is a natural way to be."

-Benjamin Zephaniah

It has been said that one in ten people have dyslexia. However, I believe that figure may be a lot more, as there are many people who are undiagnosed. For an undiagnosed dyslexic, the effect on their life can manifest itself in many different ways. For me, I experienced all the effects of undiagnosed dyslexia, such as low self-esteem, lack of confidence, early underachievement, stress and anxiety. I have had them all!

The British Dyslexia Association describes dyslexia as a neurological difference which can have a significant impact on a child's ability to grasp information and can affect their education, their employment, and the effective performance of everyday tasks. (British Dyslexia Association, 2019).

Everyone will have their own experience, and each will be different, as everyone is unique, and no two dyslexics are the same. Dyslexia is hereditary and can be present without being identified due to a lack of awareness or diagnosis. Dyslexia and dyspraxia are invisible, and others may not be aware of the daily struggles in performing simple tasks, such as recording information correctly, forgetting simple instructions and difficulties in time management, which can often result in missed appointments or double-booking. Having a diagnosis doesn't mean there is anything wrong, as people with these traits often excel in all areas of their lives with understanding and the right support.

Dyslexics can be great entrepreneurs – that's a word I still cannot spell! Research has found that 40 per cent of entrepreneurs and self-made millionaires are dyslexic. I love watching *Dragons' Den*, and I was proud to find out that both Peter Jones and Theo Paphitis are dyslexic and are proud of their gift. Other great entrepreneurs like Richard Branson have praised the gift of dyslexia for their great skills and the positive aspects that have contributed to their success.

As each person is unique, so is their experience of dyslexia or dyspraxia. However, I was blessed with both. Some people have one or the other or both, along with other traits such as dyscalculia, which is difficulty with numbers and understanding them. Numbers have always been a massive downfall for me, all through my life, and I am convinced that I am also dyscalculic, as I have never been able to understand maths. My mind switches off, and I have a fear of numbers.

Dyslexia can range from mild to severe, and as I don't do things by halves, my blessing came abundantly – I was diagnosed as being severely dyslexic. These traits are hereditary, so the chances are, if your parent or other family members have it, you could too.

Dyslexia is often identified in primary school or even earlier. However, some people's coping strategies are so good that their difficulties with dyslexia go unnoticed until much later in life, perhaps at secondary school or even in university or the workplace.

Research by (Kaplan et al., 1998) suggested that dyslexia and dyspraxia are intricately linked, and the study stated that 52 per cent of people with dyslexia also have similar traits to dyspraxia.

Dyslexia is not something that goes away; you have to own it and be grateful you have a gift unique to you, a superpower that can serve you in many wonderful ways. You just have to find your strengths and build them up to be the best you can be in all that you do.

What is dyspraxia?

"Dyspraxia has caused me to become resilient, hardworking and determined. It empowered me to become an encourager – I have constantly had to encourage and motivate myself and I often do it for others around me."

-Tumi Sotire, The Black Dyspraxic

Like many, I didn't know what dyspraxia was, let alone how to spell it. This word was very foreign to me, and I am just about able to spell it now. In recent years, a lot more work has been done, and people are finally understanding the true meaning of what it is and the greatness of having it. Through awareness, more people are being diagnosed every day worldwide, while many still don't have any understanding of it. I am hoping that this book will also create more awareness of it.

I was that clumsy child in every sense growing up, and even now, as an adult, I still experience challenges in my day-to-day life. Dyspraxia is an invisible condition, so it can often be missed or mistaken for something else, and it is just as common as dyslexia. It's a condition described as a developmental coordination disorder, so it can affect physical movements and the mental processing of information. Individuals with dyspraxia can struggle to organise their thoughts and understand things. Personally, timekeeping and planning daily activities are challenges I have endured all my life, along with constantly dropping things and not being able to catch a ball. These are simple things that others do effortlessly, but I can't do them. My coordination is non-existent, and as for following choreographed movements, that is definitely a no. Coordinated movements are not my thing!

Throughout my life, I wondered why I was never able to move like other people and do things like they could. For me, coordinated movement was always difficult, and I was often called clumsy and lazy, as I could never move as fast or in a coordinated way like others. I was never good at following directions, and when it came to things like dancing, I always wondered why I couldn't follow the steps in Zumba classes, as I always ended up going the wrong way from everyone else or would even trip over! While I struggled with following instructions when dancing, I know I am a good dancer (well, I think I am!). I often trip over my own feet and am terrible at stairs. Using escalators can be a challenge, and I often trip up getting on or off, as my judgement is always out of sync. It affects my driving in a big way, and I would often hesitate as spaces always look smaller than they actually are.

There are early signs that can be seen in children that need to be monitored as they grow up to ensure an early diagnosis of dyslexia and dyspraxia. Some symptoms can be similar, making it difficult to identify which learning difference they are experiencing. Signs to look out for:

- A history of reading and writing difficulties in the family
- Avoiding reading and complaining that reading is hard.
- Having difficulty associating letters with sounds
- Difficulty in sounding out simple words.
- Not recognising rhyming patterns
- The child could be labelled as clumsy and lazy.
- Frustrations when doing something they struggle with, such as maths
- Difficulty with numbers
- Difficulty in following instructions
- Lack of confidence
- Difficulty in organising thoughts while being disorganised.

- Being unmotivated
- Taking longer than others to complete a simple task.

The simple fact is I don't want people to feel what I have felt, but it's something that needs talking about, especially in our Black communities, due to so many people being dyslexic and not even knowing it. If I had been diagnosed at an early age, it would have saved me from a lot of judgement, feelings of uselessness, inadequacy, lack of confidence and task avoidance – the list goes on and on!

How I feel Inside.

I have to start with a lyric from a song by Chronixx, a well-known Jamaican singer, who is one of my absolute favourites. Many people can relate to this song, and for me, it goes like this: "You see me smile, but you don't know what I feel inside."

So many people look at me now and see this strong woman doing so much and putting the best outside, day in day out. But, like many others, I have my own personal challenges. To name a few, I am a Jamaican woman who came to England as a child and has overcome many obstacles to get where I am today.

While I now know that I was living with undiagnosed learning differences, I didn't know much about them at the time. I just knew that there was an issue with me because I was masking everything I was going through. Why was I struggling so much? Why did I feel so useless and unworthy? Why couldn't I do simple tasks or take simple instructions? It wasn't as if my job was rocket science. Things shouldn't have been that hard.

I would often over think things which caused me more complications. My brain is always going a million miles an hour. My desk was messy, just like my brain. When completing tasks, my computer would have a million and one tabs opened at the same time, just like what was going on in my brain. This was embarrassing, but that was part of me.

I felt stupid living with emotions that got the best of me each day. I was angry and dissatisfied, and I didn't know why. I was carrying all the emotions of uselessness. I couldn't organise myself or my time. Avoiding tasks and forgetting important things came easily for me, for example, walking into the edge of my desk and forgetting how the bruise got there.

How could I be a grown woman and not know my left from my right, or know which way to turn the steering wheel to park up straight, or even be able to follow instructions to get to my destination?

I carried the dark shame of not knowing who I was or why I did things the way I did.

I felt stuck and useless with people around me who I felt were better than me, another lie I told myself. All through my life, I suffered with imposter syndrome. In the workplace, when I worked for the local government, I would go to meetings in places like the House of Commons, and I would sit there and wonder why I was there because I didn't feel like I belonged. I didn't feel like I was clever or good enough to be rubbing shoulders with these people. After all, I saw myself as just a little girl from Slipe, St. Elizabeth, Jamaica, who got beaten for not knowing her times' tables.

When I finally left my job, it was like a weight lifted from my life. The terror I felt walking through those doors every morning and the feeling of I am not good enough for the job left me feeling numb. For the first time, I felt free. The unseen shackles were released.

I was glad to be finally following my dreams of achieving my degree, and as much as I loved my job in local government, it was slowly killing off my dreams and passions.

I was scared and worried because studying wouldn't be easy as it would bring out all my challenges, but it was worth it because finally, I was doing something for me as the job was making me sick every day.

I was suffering from depression and anxiety with all the masking I was doing, as I was so scared of someone discovering all my flaws and inadequacies. I didn't want to show my vulnerability because I was ashamed. I was stupid and lazy, or that was what others would think of me.

I honestly believe everything happens for a reason because if I hadn't quit my job, I would not have made the most significant discovery of my life, which helped me understand who I was and my purpose. Because I had left school without any GCSEs, I had to start from the bottom, so doing a foundation degree was my starting point when I decided to leave my job, and I was so happy when I received an unconditional offer from The Manchester College.

After I got the offer, I had to apply for student finance to pay for my course. I didn't have a job anymore, so I needed money to live whilst I studied. It was very scary applying because I hate filling in forms. I kept putting it off because it was so overwhelming with all the questions. I knew that to get it done I would have to do it a little at a time, in bite size chunks.

Starting to study at the age of 38 and being a mature student wasn't going to be easy and would come with many more added challenges. I was scared and had many questions, like how I would cope with all the coursework? How would I manage my time and organise myself? How would I know how to search for information I would need to complete my assignments? I felt sick with worrying, I felt anxious and terrified at the same time. What if I failed again, like how I failed all my GCSEs? What would I do then, with no job and a family to feed? All the questions going through my mind were crippling.

I had the added stress of finding my way around campus, remembering how to find my lecture room and getting there on time. The struggle was real because when I was working, I only had one place to find and that was it.

I knew nothing about reading and interpreting journal articles, let alone how to reference them in my assignments. At the start of my first lecture, we were warned about plagiarism which frightened the hell out of me because it would have been much easier for me to copy the words and paste them into my work, but that would have led to me being thrown off the course and I didn't want that.

I was terrified because when I read anything, I didn't remember any of it, and it would take me a really long time to understand it fully and then I didn't know where to start in putting it into my own words and paraphrasing it academically. I don't even know how I passed my first assignment, which was about air pollution. I thought the whole assignment was a mess. My paragraphs were all over the place and out of sync. All the information was included to make it a good assignment; however, it was in no correct order, it was all jumbled up, but it was there. I am good with words and can often overwrite, which was something I did for each assignment. I would always be over the word count, not knowing what to take out or keep in.

I have always hated exams and when I found out I had to do two, I nearly left the course. I went home crying to my family as I dreaded the thought. I didn't know that exams were part of the course, so it was a shock that filled me with abject fear. I had no confidence in passing these exams. I had just spent 17 years in the corporate world, and each test I had undertaken in my role to progress further, I had failed.

On the day of the exam, I felt sick and because I had to spend so long reading the questions to understand them fully, I didn't have enough time to answer all the questions, so I got a really low grade which was a minimum pass. I felt terrible and was disappointed in myself.

I was relieved when I got through my first year and was offered the opportunity to do my top-up degree for another two years. I was getting closer to achieving my dream of a degree, but the other two years wouldn't be easy because I was working towards a full degree and the assignments would get even harder.

Each lecture left me drained with so much information going through my brain. I found it hard to keep up with the lecturer and copying notes was just a waste of time because it was just taking me too long as I tried to listen and write at the same time. There was too much happening at the same time. When I looked at my notes afterwards, none made sense.

Each assignment I completed, I was fearful of failing because of my jumbled-up thinking and writing. In addition, because I lacked confidence in my understanding and writing skills, I was scared of asking anyone to check my work because they would find out how poor my writing was.

I cringed at the thought of my lecturer reading my work. I managed to pass each assignment with a good grade. However, my feedback would be long, pointing out areas of improvement. This would bring on more anxiety and worry for the next assignment.

I looked forward to half term and study weeks as I would get a break from studying without worrying about going to lectures, but then the anxiety would kick in. Then, I was filled with dread when it was time to go back.

I got involved in activities that would take my mind off studying and was both student representative and student ambassador for the whole three years that I was there. I enjoyed being a voice for others as it involved a lot of verbal communication, which was something I was really good at doing. The meetings were great; they allowed me to help change things and make our study experience better for all. The meetings didn't involve taking notes, so that was great.

I had no idea that the last year of my degree would give me the answers I was looking for. I wanted to make more of an effort because my final year would determine my overall grade for my degree.

I developed a great relationship with Lesley, one of the librarians on our UCEN campus. We always have a little chat and she often told me to come and ask her if I needed help. Unfortunately, I didn't have the courage to ask her for help until I completed the last assignment before I had to do my dissertation.

I was reluctant to ask her for help as she would see all my writing faults. However, the deadline was fast approaching, so I had to grit my teeth and email it to her. I finally sent it, but I was worried about what she would find and all the work I would have to do after she checked it. When she emailed back to me, I was scared of opening it and just as I thought, it was full of changes that I needed to make, and they were all highlighted in yellow.

I was shocked at all the words that were spelt incorrectly, but there was a big reason for that. I found out that the spell checker on my laptop wasn't working. After looking over the assignment, I went to the library to see Lesley. I was shocked at what came out of her mouth. You could have knocked me down with a feather when she said to me, "I didn't know you were dyslexic. I have a brother who is dyslexic, and I noticed the similarity in your work." Well, this was the moment I felt like a light was beaming down on me through the roof and everything started to become clear as this revelation was the start of my journey of discovery. I had always heard the term dyslexia, but I didn't even think it was something I had. My friend Valerie had it, but I just didn't associate myself with it.

Lesley advised me to contact Student Support Services and speak to someone about it, which I did straight away, as I only had a few weeks left there, so if I wanted to be assessed it would need to be done before I finished my degree.

I went to see Student Support Services; they were very helpful and supportive. They agreed to pay for my assessment which lasted over 3 hours. Following that, I received a report from the assessor, which stated that I had severe dyslexia and dyspraxia.

By this time, I had to start working on my dissertation, which meant I was close to finishing my degree. I was overwhelmed, and I started to procrastinate, but with the help of my supervisor, I finally made a start.

It was the biggest and last piece of work I had to complete before I could say I was finished. This was really hard because there were so many different elements to it. I was terrified of starting the process and overwhelmed by it all. First, I had to choose a topic to research; then I had to find willing participants. I chose the topic of fibromyalgia and managed to find seven participants who had the condition. Once I had interviewed them, I had to write it all up whilst ensuring it was logical and made sense. Again, it was a big struggle, and I knew the importance of completing it to a high standard as it would contribute to my final grade.

Because I had received my dyslexia diagnosis, I was able to access extra support and had the option of requesting extra time to complete it. I worked hard with my supervisor and completed it on time to meet my deadline. It was such a relief the day I handed it in. It was definitely one of the biggest highlights of my studies. I did it and I was really proud of myself.

After receiving my diagnosis whilst working on my dissertation, I had no time to deal with all the emotions and frustrations that came with the diagnosis. Inside I felt crushed, but I had to continue working hard, regardless. I remember crying myself to sleep many nights and I noticed that the stress was severely affecting my mood.

When I finished all my work and finally had time to think about my diagnosis and everything I had gone through, I felt a sense of relief with mixed emotions. There were so many questions going around in my head, like what if the spell checker was working for that assignment and Lesley didn't get to see all the incorrect spellings? I wouldn't have been assessed.

My emotions were all over the place, and I was frustrated because I had so many questions, worries, and fears about my life from a noticeably young age and throughout my teenage and adult life, which led to feelings of uselessness, worthlessness, and not being good enough, which led to low self-esteem and lack of confidence.

Whilst I had a sense of relief, I felt incredibly low. I felt cheated and let down by my school, college and workplace. They should have seen it coming; why didn't they investigate further why I was confronted with so many obstacles and experienced such a wide range of difficulties?

The whole system had let me down and I felt a deep sense of neglect and sadness. I was just left to suffer in silence and that wasn't good.

I was dyslexic and dyspraxic, conditions which I knew nothing about. That was why I learned and did things differently. That was why I have so much empathy for others, that's why I am such a great communicator and connector with a passion for helping others. Yet, underneath all the challenges, I possessed great qualities and knew this but didn't always remember it.

I became angry with myself for all the negative feelings that manifested from not knowing who I was and why I was different from everyone else in so many ways.

I was on an emotional rollercoaster, I felt alone but finally, I had the answers and the realisation that I wasn't stupid, I wasn't thick, I wasn't a dunce and that all the negative labels that I accepted were not true, I had learning differences like many others around the world.

All my life, I had developed strategies that helped to hide the challenges but finally, I was on a journey of understanding and acceptance. I had to own it and understand that this is part of me and my superpower. I had to embrace it.

Now, I knew why I couldn't spell to save my life, or pronounce certain words, why I couldn't follow simple instructions, why I struggled to remember people's names, why I was so forgetful, why I couldn't manage my time or organise myself, why my life was so chaotic, why I couldn't tell my left from my right, why I get so overwhelmed and tired with too much information, why I couldn't organise my work, why my writing was all over the place, why I couldn't express my thoughts clearly and concisely, why I double book myself, why I missed appointments. The list is endless.

From this revelation, I was confused. I wanted to talk to my parents about it, but they knew nothing about dyslexia or dyspraxia. I was depressed because I feared people would perceive and judge me differently. They were unaware of how brilliant people with learning differences can be and that there is nothing wrong with me; I just learn and think differently.

Following my diagnosis, I started to do my own research on dyslexia and dyspraxia. I read several articles which said that there were close links to learning differences and issues with mental health, something which I've never spoken about openly. I was very sure that when I lost my grandma in my teens, which was my first encounter with depression, but it was nothing I knew much about.

It wasn't until later on in my life I started to understand more about it, as this is something that is not usually discussed in our communities. Because for a long-time mental health issues were not taken seriously, or you would be labelled as being mad. With all my existing labels, which I had believed about myself, I didn't want to add this to my list, but I know on my journey, my mental health was always at its best.

It all made sense, why I would often get moody and have angry outbursts from all the frustrations I had bottled up all these years. It was a mental struggle each day.

Along with the challenges, I also found all the evidence I needed that proved the greatness of being neurodiverse, so I knew that I had to surround myself with other people who also had Dyslexia and Dyspraxia because they would understand what I was going through. We had that common bond of our lived experiences.

The response I got when I started to tell people was mixed as some people felt sorry for me and some thought that something was wrong with me. This was upsetting and frustrating trying to convince others there was nothing wrong with me. Their reactions sent me back to that dark place where I didn't want to be.

I remember reaching out to a family member to tell them about my diagnosis and their response was terribly negative and I was very upset when they said I was deficient as a person. This was the worst thing they could have said to me because I was extremely sensitive and vulnerable at the time.

Things changed when I started to be more open about accepting who I was, which was when I started connecting with more people like me on social media. I found LinkedIn to be a great place of comfort as there were so many other neurodiverse people sharing great content. My network quickly grew, and I developed the courage to share my story with whoever would listen.

When I started to open up, the invitations started rolling in to share my story and then more and more people were reaching out to me to talk about their own stories. I also found out that several people in my own family also had dyslexia and dyspraxia, which I didn't know about and because of the lack of awareness, shame and ignorance that exists, especially in the Black community, many people were suffering in silence. Like myself, they didn't want others to see or think of them differently. In those moments, I promised myself, my children, and generations to come that my mission would be to create more awareness locally and globally, so I decided to write a book to share my story and empower other dyslexics.

After finishing my degree, I wondered whether I wanted to continue studying. However, I was very much in two minds as I was tired and drained mentally, physically and emotionally.

I was struggling to make the decision, so after a good chat with my lecturer Geoff Bowling, once I received results and found out that I had achieved a First-Class Honours Degree in Applied Science and Exercise. I decided to go ahead. I started to look at the Masters in Health that was available at Manchester Metropolitan University. I knew it wouldn't be easy, but it was naturally the next step of progression for me. Not in a million years did I think I would be doing a Masters, this was a big deal, a very big deal. I was always interested in psychology and the brain, so I decided on a Masters in health psychology as one of the modules was on Neurophysiology.

The University had an open day which I attended as I needed to know if sitting exams was part of the course. I was relieved when the course leader reassured me that no exams were involved.
I applied, got accepted, and even got a ten percent

discount as I had achieved a First-Class Honours on my degree.

My diagnosis meant I would get support from the Student Disability Service. I contacted them with my diagnosis report, and they helped me to claim for Disability Student Allowance (DSA). After a few weeks wait, I received a letter from them informing me that I was eligible for a support worker to help me with my work, plus equipment such as a laptop and assistive technology. This was great, but I was anxious about starting a Masters. The first day I stepped through the doors of the Birley Fields Campus, I was still wondering if I had made the right decision. Everyone was lovely and friendly, but I found the building overwhelming, with tall ceilings and huge stairways.

The lectures were different, with a lot more information to take in as there were more modules which were very different from my BSc degree. However, all the other students seem to be so knowledgeable as their previous studies were in psychology.

I was very open from the start about having dyslexia and when I found out that other students on my course had it too, that made things easier as I was able to use my assistive technology in each lecture without them wondering what I was doing when I sat there recording each presentation. I really found it useful to use the Sonocent note taker to record all my lecture notes.

Whilst I was getting better support, I was struggling because the workload was more intense, and the journal articles were more difficult to understand. I was absolutely dreading the first assignment as I started to doubt my ability to take on a Masters. The imposter syndrome was kicking in again. The first few months were really hard as I had panic attacks which no one knew about, not even my family.

After starting my master's in late September, there was a threat of the COVID-19 pandemic. Unfortunately, by March everything changed, and we were all in lockdown, which meant that we weren't allowed to have lectures on campus and our course had to be taught online. This was difficult for me because I couldn't keep up with all the online information and navigate many different files and folders.

My first assessment was in April, and we had to do the exam online by recording a video and uploading it in an exam style setting. On the day of the assessment, I was in tears as I knew I wasn't going to pass it and thought I'd failed my first assignment. Even with the extra time I was given, it just wasn't enough. Everyone else had passed and I failed it by two marks. I was devastated. I spoke to my lecturers and told them how I found it difficult. They reassured me that the exam this assessment was in two parts and that as long as I passed the second part of it, I would pass it overall.

I was struggling and couldn't sleep at night and became really depressed. I went to my doctor, who took some blood tests and the results showed that I had no iron or serotonin in my body. So he prescribed anti-depressants and another tablet to increase my serotonin levels, but I couldn't take either of them because they made me nauseous and lightheaded. There were days when I felt numb, I had lost all enjoyment in everything. It was a difficult time, as there were days when I would curl up on the sofa in my blanket and cry. I didn't want to do anything or see anyone. I was emotional all the time.

Everyone sees me as this strong woman doing all these amazing things, so only my family, Natalie, Bexx, my personal tutor and my support worker knew what I was going through at the time.

My doctor sent me a referral to go to North Trafford Hospital for an iron transfusion, which made me feel better for a few weeks, but I still couldn't take the antidepressants.

I started my own research and found out that pineapples were good for producing serotonin in the body, so I started to eat plenty of pineapples and every day, I went out for long walks and drank plenty of water which really helped. I am so grateful to the people that knew what I was going through and were there for me.

This time I couldn't hide it because it was showing up in everything I did. The low mood, crying, and lack of motivation to do anything were too obvious to hide.

Doing my radio show on a Sunday helped too, as it was a way of me escaping what I was going through as I love music, so I felt better when I listened.

Whilst all this was going on, many people were getting COVID-19, going into hospital and dying. So, it was a harrowing time for everyone.

For the remainder of my Masters, I got great support from my study buddies, my family and my friends, who knew about what I was going through. It wasn't easy because many times I thought I wouldn't get through it and wanted to give up, but my dyslexic resilience wouldn't let me.

One of the hardest things was doing a Masters during a pandemic. I still don't know how I got through it, but I finished it and achieved a merit. You can get through anything when you have great people and support.

I am dyslexic, I am dyspraxic and I am Blessed and Gifted!

One of my biggest motivations to carry was the day my Queen, my eldest Daughter told me, "Mummy, I am so proud of you." I knew she was inspired by all that I was doing and that I was her inspiration when we graduated a week apart from the same university. That was a beautiful day when she also graduated with a First-Class Honours Degree in International Business and Marketing.

Those words meant a lot to me, as I know she has had her own challenges and has seen all my good and bad days.

The biggest lesson I have learnt is don't worry about what others think of me, be easy on myself, show myself more empathy and love, learn to accept, recognise and celebrate the great work I am doing to change the narrative from shame, embarrassment, and ignorance.

Everyone sees the successes of people with dyslexia, but they don't see all the challenges we face behind closed doors. I still have days now when I don't want to do anything, but it's not because I am lazy; it's because I am human and at times, I need to rest my brain and look after me because there is just one me and I am uniquely me.

Even while writing this book, I was struggling. I started to be hard on myself, worrying if it was good enough, would anyone buy it? Would anyone read it? Would they understand any of it? So many questions swirling around in my head. I was doing it again, doubting myself and my abilities. I find that when I am overthinking, the best thing is to talk to someone who understands me and knows what I am going through, so I knew what I had to do. After a long chat with my publisher Marcia and several voice notes from my friend, who is also called Marcia, I was reminded how far I have come on my journey and how amazing I am in all that I do. These ladies really helped me in putting things into perspective.

If you are reading this and you know someone who is neurodiverse, be patient with them because they will be dealing with things that you don't even know about. Give them love, patience, support and be kind to them.

Be kind, as you never know what others are going through because we don't walk with a label on our forehead saying what we are going through in life!

"Each person with dyslexia and dyspraxia will come with a set of skills that, if recognised and harnessed, can make them the best they can and want to be."

- Professor Amanda Kirby,
CEO of Do-IT Solutions

My unknown condition in Jamaica.

My school days were colourful. If you have been to Jamaica, you may know more about our little island and how different it is from England. While I had the sunshine and the sky, my own sun wasn't shining as bright as it should. I had a cloud which I carried around with me, and it was something I didn't know about and, today, many still don't.

I felt so much pain in school, day in and day out. Every day was a struggle, and I felt stupid all the time, not knowing why things didn't add up.

If the UK still has a long way to go in dealing with learning differences, you can just imagine how far behind Jamaica is when it comes to understanding conditions such as dyslexia, dyspraxia, and dyscalculia. So many children have slipped through the net and will never know what caused their struggles in life, especially in school and often in later life too.

My most feared subject in school was maths, and I am sure that my 'math dyslexia' was the cause of that. It looks like I have been blessed with most of these learning differences, and dyscalculia was the cause of my struggles with maths. Being confused by simple maths and numbers was frustrating.

I would eventually get the answer, but it would take me much longer than anyone else because my head would get muddled up with remembering the correct number or sequence. When my great-grandparents sent me to the shop, I would never know if I had been given the wrong change, as my focus was never on numbers, and I hated anything that involved them. My father was the same, and the only person I remember being good at numbers was my great-grandad Brooks or Aaron, which was his actual name. I was always so confused about what was happening around me and would get very worried about things I wasn't familiar with.

Any embarrassing situation you can think of has happened to me, from spilling my lunch to burning my hand in the canteen with hot curry sauce; the pain was unbearable, and today, I still have the scar on the back of my hand. When I was growing up in Jamaica, I questioned myself a lot, as I couldn't understand why it took me so long to learn or do things. Why could they ride a bicycle, and I couldn't? I really wanted to learn, but I was so scared I wouldn't be able to do it. I did learn to ride a bicycle; however, it was at the cost of hurting myself several times over and over again, and I have a clear memory of ending up headfirst in a lamppost in front of everyone. I will never forget that day, as it was right in front of my primary school, just across the road from the house where my mom lived after we lost everything in Hurricane Gilbert in 1988.

That was one of the most difficult times in my life. We had to depend on handouts of food and clothes from abroad. It was exciting to get things from abroad, but for me, it didn't turn out very well, as expected. I really thought I would have got more on the day; however, because I was awfully slow and couldn't move as fast as everyone else due to my clumsiness, other people got all the good stuff, and I missed out on the nicer things. Everyone pushed past me to grab what they wanted. I remember feeling really sad and disappointed with myself for not getting anything good.

Growing up, I was very clumsy, to the point where I would trip and fall over things all the time, even over nothing, just my own feet. I remember being really slow in doing and understanding things, but I was good at running and always won on sports day, as I was fast. Tripping up and falling over was always going to happen, so my daily dose of embarrassment was a sure thing. Doing normal, everyday things was a big struggle. When we were out playing, my lack of judgement always took over, and I was the last one to complete any task that involved instructions. I was very good at taking instructions, but soon after, I would forget all about them. My memory often gets me into trouble. Forgetting things is a daily thing for me!

While I love books, I didn't learn to read until extremely late, and I remember the feeling of relief when I realised, I knew what certain words were. It was such a great moment, with a feeling of great satisfaction.

When we played cricket, and it came to choosing a team, I was terrified of being picked to be a fielder, as I couldn't catch the ball due to my lack of coordination. However, I wasn't any better at bowling, as I was never able to get the ball to go in the right direction so it could be hit with the bat. I would often see the ball coming but couldn't catch it, no matter how hard I tried, so I would end up getting hit.

Growing up in Jamaica meant we didn't have many books, but I loved them. Whenever I got hold of a book, I would read it over and over, as I couldn't remember what I had just read. Our lack of books meant we found other ways of learning. One way was to explore the beautiful land we had around us, so as children, we got up to all sorts. Jamaica is a beautiful country, and we wasted no time when it came to exploring our surroundings.

Evenings were fun as that was when we would get up to no good, and I mean no good in every sense. We were inquisitive, and if there was anything happening, we would have to be involved in it. Wherever there was sugar cane or a fruit tree, we would find it. If we knew that a certain land had ripe fruits, we would be there picking and eating them. We would eat so much on the way back from school that, when we reached home, we would be already full up, with no room for dinner. My favourite was mango, any type of mango, and as kids, we sold mangoes and cashews, but my big problem was counting them. I always got mixed up with the amounts. I would always get excited when it was cashew time because, believe it or not, we had the pleasure of picking cashews. I love cashews, even to this day. I don't think many people even know how they are grown or that they grow on something we called 'cashew meat.' It's a fleshy fruit, and when it's ripe, it's very tasty. The cashew meat makes a tasty jam, too.

My Grandma Bertha was always in her element when it came to cashew time, and I wondered how she managed to gather so many cashews in such a short time, but this was due to my concept of numbers. She was very good at counting them; however, I never heard her read, and I don't think she ever learnt. I believe so many people that never learnt to read and write growing up didn't get the help and support they needed, so they have truly missed out on reaching their full potential in life. My grandma and many others went through this, and the lack of understanding of these conditions in Jamaica didn't help.

The counting and adding up that I didn't understand, and the lashings with the leather strap at school for not knowing my times' tables, was enough to put me off maths for life! We used to get double if we pulled our hand away. Many that grew up in the Caribbean will understand. We had a teacher from hell! Every day was difficult and imagine being beaten for not knowing your times' tables. Our teacher wasn't an ordinary teacher. This man ate red herring and crackers every day without fail. He would drink up the rum from Larry Dunkley's shop and was so feisty at times that he would send us to buy his food! Yes, after beating us in the morning, he would ask one of us to go to the shop to get his lunch and snacks! He always had a strong smell of rum! That rum smell was a strong clue to what mood he would be in that day and how angry he would be. We were always terrified of going to class, which triggered my fear of maths.

Our schoolbooks had the times' tables on the back, so we had no excuse for not knowing them, but that didn't help me as I couldn't understand, no matter how hard I tried. I didn't know how to get around the situation. I used to count on my fingers, but when other people were able to do their times tables on their fingers, I couldn't. I would even count my toes when I ran out of fingers. I gave up on the fact that I would eventually learn it. I would often think that people called me slow for a good reason, and I started to believe it.

English wasn't bad, and in Miss Scott's class, I made sure I sat next to either one of my bright cousins, Sasha or Sasheen. I could always depend on them because they understood what was being taught, unlike me, so I knew they would help and let me copy their work if I needed to. Copying was not always a good thing because if they got it wrong, I would also get it wrong, and I didn't know whether their work was right or not. Everything in class seemed to go so fast that I could never keep up, especially with copying from the board, which meant I would miss notes and was always the last one to finish. I loved school and tried to go as much as I could, and even when some kids didn't go, I made sure I went, with or without lunch money. My mom lived near the school, just across the road, to be precise, so if I didn't have lunch, I could always go there for something to eat.

I could always rely on Auntie Elena, who was so kind to us. She was very clever and helped us many times with our homework. Boy, we had some fun, but I remember I was clumsy to the point where sometimes I was called "one-handed," "idiat", or "stupid". On Fridays, when many didn't bother going to school, I did because I was so scared of missing things and having to catch up.

Miss Scott was a great teacher, but she went amazingly fast – so fast that I struggled to keep up. She was my cousin and knew my family well.

I never had much confidence growing up and was the cowardly one. Some jokes were also at my expense, and I remember my cousin tied me to a cow that ran off. That was just one of my close calls. I remember almost being killed in the town of Middle Quarters, when my daddy saved me from being hit by a car. I saw him coming from across the road and ran over to him on a terribly busy corner. It was an awfully close call; the car missed me by an inch. I am grateful to be alive today. Due to my lack of judgement, I thought the car was far away, and I could get across the road quickly enough. My daddy remembers it well and reminded me of the incident when he visited the UK in 2014.

Growing up, my daddy could only read a little and didn't go far in his education as he wasn't interested in school. Most learning conditions are common in Jamaica, but because of the lack of understanding of learning differences, only a few people are aware. Daddy didn't have any qualifications, but he was truly knowledgeable; he often told me stories and taught me many life lessons. He always believed in me and knew that I was special. I was eager to learn, so I tried my best every day! Daddy really wanted me to do well and would make sure I went to school every day, and he would save any money he had for my lunch money. He was always positive about life and encouraged me to look on the bright side.

Dyslexia is thought to be hereditary, and that is definitely a fact in my family, so I owe it to my children to pay close attention to their learning styles and how they are developing. So many children have slipped through the net in Jamaica because teachers and parents don't know about these conditions, and there is no support to help them. They will continue to slip through the net, as schools in Jamaica don't put a lot of focus on learning differences. I choose to call it a learning difference, as it's not a difficulty and more of a gift and blessing. Many are still ignorant of the issues of these learning differences.

It runs in the family.

My great-grandad couldn't read or write, but no one could beat him at maths. Unfortunately, I didn't take that from him, as maths was and is my worst nightmare. Even when we tried to outsmart him with money, he was a very clever man and just couldn't be fooled. His memory was something else; no one could ever owe him money and not pay it back. I remember his daughter, the late Aunt Zandra, and I tried to trick him. We hid $10 from him to buy aerated water, which was what they called soft drinks back then. We thought we had gotten away with it, but he counted every penny and found that $10 was missing. Back then, $10 was worth a lot more than it is now. I was always fascinated by my great-grandad's understanding of maths, but I couldn't understand it at all. I am sure it must have crossed his mind at some point – what is wrong with this child? Why does she find it so hard? He was patient with me and cared for my education. He always boasted about me, and anything I achieved, he would tell everyone.

When the time came for me to go to high school, I was worried I wasn't bright enough to get good grades and get into a high class. I used to look at the brighter girls in my district and thought I wasn't good enough as they were brighter than me, or so I thought. They got into the high schools outside our district that I wanted to go to, and I used to hear of other students passing their entry exams to go to high school. I wanted that badly and wanted to get in with a good grade, and that's when I realised you can achieve whatever you put your mind to. I went for the test to get into Lacovia High School when I was thirteen and was surprised. I managed to get into 8/2 – not quite the top class, but 8/2 wasn't bad at all, as the top class was 8/1. I was so happy with myself for getting in at that level as I thought that was unreachable for me. I don't even know how I got through the exam, as I hated exams. Whenever I was faced with one, I would worry that I wouldn't be able to do it.

I was terrified of missing school and made sure I went every day, whether I had lunch money or not. My daddy did his best to make sure I had money to go to school, but I knew if he didn't have it, my mom lived just across the road from the school, so I would get lunch if she had it.

I have always been a daydreamer, but I had a fear factor attached as I would convince myself I couldn't do something, so I would get scared of trying. Just like when I was determined to learn to ride a bike and ended up crashing headfirst into a lamppost. I learnt to ride, and the crash was worth it (no pain, no gain)!

Key take away

"Creativity, perseverance is what we are."

-Lena Arday, creative, fellow dyslexic

Never think you cannot achieve anything in life. If you are determined enough, despite the challenges you will come across, keep going. Never believe you are not good enough or that anyone is better than you. There is someone out there wishing they could do the things you can do, so always have faith and remember that we are all unique in our own way!

My determination started from an early age and carried me a long way, regardless of my struggles – that is what life is all about. We will have struggles and challenges, but we need to be resilient and think positively. It can be so easy to see the worst in every situation, but if we look deeper, there is always an experience to be learnt. It may not seem like it at the time, but when the situation passes, you will look back and see that it wasn't so bad after all. Positivity goes a long way and will always help.

My Journey Into the Unknown!

"The long-lasting dreams placed in your heart are yours to fulfil. The people that didn't believe in you. Prove them wrong."

-Keisha Swaby (my own quote)

My destiny was laid out for me to come to the UK, and the dream became a reality. With that came the biggest change that would shape my life and show me what I have been blessed with.

I always knew I was a little slow in understanding things, but I am definitely not dumb! However, I believed that I was for a very long time.

Coming to England was a dream, and I had the belief that I would get there one day. I would often daydream about the cold and imagine what it would be like. I had only ever heard about it or seen it on TV. I didn't know how at that time, but when God has a plan for you, things will just fall into place. For me, that's what happened – everything clicked. When my grandma and auntie came to Jamaica to visit in 1991, it was a dream come true, as I have always longed to meet them. Daddy always told me his mother, sister, and other relatives lived in England. I didn't know then that their trip would be part of the plan which would fulfil my dream to go there. Grandma always made me feel great about myself, and I fell in love with her the first time I met her. We had an incredibly special bond; she was my protector and was very fair with people, so she had a way of making them feel special. She loved her children and grandchildren, and that made me feel secure.

I remember arriving in England. My journey on the flight was something else. I still have the black handbag I came with and remember the brown skirt suit I wore on the flight. It's not something I would wear now, but at the time, I thought I looked hot. I was so nervous about travelling on my own and was scared – I mean really scared. The airport was something else, and I was terrified of getting on the wrong flight, and at the time, I was very shy. Imagine boarding a flight in Montego Bay in a full suit; I was boiling hot. No one knew, but I was so frightened about catching a flight all the way to England on my own. I knew I had to ask questions, but it wasn't easy asking them as I felt they wouldn't understand my deep Jamaican accent. I kept looking at the screens to see when my flight was ready, but I really struggled reading off the screen to see when my flight would be boarding and from which gate. I plucked up the courage and asked another passenger, and when I found out she was on the same flight as me, I stuck to her like glue. I watched her every move, and everything she did, I did the same. In fact, I was so glued to her that I even followed her to the toilet, which is funny looking back. It was the only way to make sure I didn't lose her.

I travelled on British Airways to Gatwick. I was overwhelmed by the size of the airport when I got there, as it was very big and overwhelming. I wasn't sure what I needed to do when I got there. It was an exciting journey, but I was also terrified of the whole process. Once I got on the flight, it got a bit easier as I had the help of an air hostess. She was lovely and really helped me.

I have heard of people not being able to get through immigration, and when I got there, I was so scared of them questioning me. At that moment, when it came to my turn in the long line, I didn't know whether they would question me about why I was going to the UK, so I kept quiet and only spoke when spoken to. I didn't want to say too much, in the hope they wouldn't question me more. I made it through, and it was a great feeling when I saw my grandma and auntie waiting on the other side to greet me. I felt such a great sense of relief because, trust me, I was sweating after I left the immigration desk. Many people will relate to the ordeal of going through immigration, not knowing whether you are going to be let in (yeah, the immigration sweat!). The immigration officer didn't know it, but I knew I wouldn't be going back to Jamaica after the six months they stamped in my passport. I didn't know how I would get to stay in the country, but I knew I was here to stay.

One of my biggest challenges was starting school in the UK. I was fourteen, so I only had two years left in high school. Starting school in a new country wasn't easy. I just wanted to fit in, but I didn't know how.

I knew that all the other children would be ahead of me, and more than likely, they would understand all they were being taught better than me. The classes they placed me in were so different to what I was used to back in Jamaica. Each class scared me, and I knew keeping up with the teacher was going to be hard. Their accents seemed so strong, and I felt stupid asking them over and over to repeat what was said, so in the end, I stopped asking, which led to me missing key information.

I hated PE and was always embarrassed by the amount of time it would take me to change and get ready for it. Changing times were embarrassing, and dropping things while getting ready was a regular thing for me. I loved netball and was good at it. I played in goal attack and would bump into other players and walk into things, so I'd be covered in bruises. Bruises were a regular thing for me, and at times I would just notice them on my body without remembering how I got them! I fell all the time, especially when playing certain games. Anything which involved me catching a ball always resulted in injuries.

I loved netball in Jamaica and was glad when I got on the netball team when I joined the school. I had a good height, which was useful, but I had the worst coordination on the court, and falling over was a regular thing. I spent more time falling over than standing up, and I was the laughingstock of the team. If it were a case of scoring clumsiness, I would have definitely won each game. My aunt was forever buying me items for my PE kit, as each week, I would lose something in the changing room – forgetting things was another major challenge.

I really struggled, and every day, I wished I was back in Jamaica, where I knew everyone in my class, and everyone knew me. I was behind everyone, and there was no way I could catch up to their level, as they understood what they were being taught. I felt worse off than my classmates, and I depended on them in class, as they always knew the answers. God help me if they got it wrong because so would I, and I often got them wrong from copying. Not everyone's handwriting is readable, so copying is not always a good thing. Copying maths was the hardest part, as I struggled to make out the numbers and never understood how they got to the answer, so if I was ever asked how I got to the answer, I could never explain it.

I got anxious if I missed school due to the fact that, when I was there, I didn't understand, so if I missed a day, it would make things worse. So, I learnt that I couldn't afford to miss a day as it would be an even bigger struggle to catch up. It was even worse when the people I copied from were off school; my heart would sink as I wouldn't have anyone to copy from.

Not wanting to miss anything is something I have carried through to every job I have had. Being there every day is something I ensured even when I was sick. I would go in because I feared the build-up of work and playing catch-up.

After spending two years in Darlaston Comprehensive school, in the West Midlands, I left school without any GCSE's. I failed them all with a big, fat "F". I wasn't surprised at all because I really struggled. I made a promise to myself that I wouldn't settle for not having any qualifications. I promised myself that, one day, I would go further with my studies. Leaving school without any qualifications wasn't easy to accept, and I remember the sadness and feelings of worthlessness.

When I went to Manchester to live after finishing school, my gran found me my first job cleaning offices near the city centre. I got lost so many times when I first started, and I would be up and down in the lift because I would get confused by each floor as they all looked the same! It took me way longer than everyone else to get my floor cleaned – it took forever. The other girls, I am sure, were fed up with me and couldn't understand what my problems were. Even emptying a bin took way too long; they would empty at least four bins while I was still on the same one.

How would I get into college, as I wasn't like any other student? I was the only one with no GCSE's! This terrified me, as I knew that without them getting into college would be a struggle. Going to university after college didn't even cross my mind, as it was something I never thought I could do at that point. I never thought I would have a love for English, but I decided I wanted to do my English again.

At that time, I didn't have a right to stay in the country, and my grandma, who was helping me sort it out, had passed away. I was lost and felt like I had no one to turn to. My whole world was upside down. Losing my gran was one of the hardest things, as I felt like my whole world had crumbled around me. My gran was someone I could talk to about anything, and I mean anything. She was amazing, with a great sense of humour. I think about her every day, and I wish she was still here now to see my own family and all my achievements. She was a big inspiration to me, and we had such a strong bond. She loved her family dearly.

My college days

another missed opportunity.

"I was dyslexic. I had no understanding of schoolwork whatsoever. I certainly would have failed IQ tests. And it was one of the reasons I left school when I was 15 years old. And if I'm not interested in something, I don't grasp it."

-Richard Branson

I didn't let my immigration status or lack of it in the country stop me from continuing with my studies. I enrolled into Loreto College, and the Lord, or whoever you believe in, carried me through. I am great at writing, but I would often switch things around or change words to make my own word. I remember sitting my English language exam at Loreto College. It was a frightening day for me as I was scared of failing. I had a great teacher called Ms

58

McQuade. I remember her helping me and explaining things. She didn't know at the time that I had dyslexia, but she would break things down in a simple way and really had time for me. She was one of those teachers that saw the best in me; she was so helpful and patient. She had a lovely way about her and how she taught which made things a lot easier for me. I am profoundly grateful for her help and support. I'm not sure where she is now, which is a shame, as I would have liked to thank her for seeing in me something I didn't see at the time. Anyway, I passed my English GCSE with a grade C. I know I could have got higher with a bit more help!

In life, you can't let challenges stop you. If you want to do something bad enough, you will find a way, and it will work out the way you want! I didn't have my stay in the country, but I didn't let that stop me! I took a risk, and it paid off. I knew the importance of education, and I wasn't going to let anything stop me! My exam was on *Educating Rita*, which I loved. From a child, I have always been a dreamer, with great storylines in my head, and it was something I thoroughly enjoyed as the characters were amazing. I loved Julie Walters in the film! I haven't seen that film in a long time, but it still makes me smile thinking about it!

Exams were never my strong point, so I remember the day I took the exam, I felt awful. I was terrified and don't know how I got through it, but I did. It must have been the fact I loved English, and that film was brilliant, so I guess, I remembered more than I thought I could.

I was so happy to pass my English GCSE. Getting that piece of paper confirming I had passed was a very joyful and emotional time. From then on, I knew I could achieve anything if I put my mind to it, and it gave me great confidence to carry on! I then went on to study a GNVQ in information technology at Loreto College. We had a great teacher, but I just couldn't get my head around the digits in programming. Of all the things to study, I chose information technology. I shouldn't have chosen that because I had a fear of numbers, so that wasn't for me at all. They say in life, a good teacher can make all the difference to your school experience, and Mr Wray was that teacher for me. He was very patient and explained things slowly when I didn't understand. He was particularly good at computers, and programming was his thing, but it wasn't mine, as I didn't understand much of it as there were too many numbers to deal with.

Everyone in the class seemed to understand except me! I was always behind when copying from the board or entering the figures on the screen! Why did I think I would get very far with something riddled with numbers? I remember sitting next to my friend, Jacqui Henderson. She and everyone else in the class got it straight away, and I kept wondering why they were so good at it, and I was struggling so much. I knew I wasn't going to be a computer programmer because it wasn't something that I could master.

I loved sitting next to Jacqui because she had the most amazing handwriting. She had what you call pretty handwriting; it was easier to copy from her as my brain didn't grasp the words quickly enough to write as fast as the others. Jacqui knew this, so she was always quick to hand me her book to complete what I missed on the board. Because my tutors nor I knew I had dyslexia and dyspraxia, nothing was ever done to support me during my time at college. It was a hard struggle as I was so easily confused and couldn't keep up in any of my classes. My understanding wasn't that quick, and I was always playing catch-up. Every day, I would miss something, and when Jacqui wasn't in, that was worse as I didn't have anyone to copy from. Everything was a constant struggle, and it was all confusing.

I didn't learn much in my classes as I felt so behind with everything. I struggled to understand things when they weren't broken down into steps. In that college, I will never forget how my clumsiness embarrassed me in front of everyone. Tripping up in the foyer was one of the most embarrassing times of my life, and it's a memory that I can never forget. There were only two stairs in my way, but that still didn't stop me from going flying. At the time, I just wanted the ground to swallow me up; it all happened in slow motion, and I felt all eyes directed at me. Stairs were never my thing, and today, I still trip up and down them. Getting on and off escalators is another story, as I constantly misjudge my steps.

Like many others, our brains take a little longer to connect to our body movements, so in the foyer, when I tripped over and was sent flying straight down the stairs in front of everyone, I felt my cheeks burning red hot from embarrassment and shame.

I would read because I love books and could easily live in a library, but despite loving books and having a passion for words, I would read and then forget what I had read. This was a massive struggle for me – how could I possibly learn if I couldn't remember what I was reading about? Everything was a blur. I wish I had known I was dyslexic while studying at Loreto College, as I am sure they would have given me the right support.

Studying at college in the nineties was great, and there were some amazing students there. The teachers were great, and I have a lot to thank them for. One of my favourite teachers was Mr Wray. He was a very patient teacher. At the time, he wouldn't have known I had dyslexia, but he broke things down when he was explaining in class, and that was significant for me, as I was able to keep up and understand it in a simple way. While writing this book, I bumped into Mr Wray in Asda, and it was really good to see him. The thing is, you never forget a good teacher and how they impacted your life.

Thanks to the teachers at Loreto College for the start in my learning journey and the start of my achievement journey. There were quite a few of us there at the time from our local community, but I was the only one that knew of my struggles. Only after connecting with other people on social media and sharing my own story did I find out they, too, had dyslexia. I was shocked to learn that Lena had dyslexia at college, as she studied art and was always so creative, which was lucky, as the college had a great art department. She now designs brilliant things from her love of creating. I can really say I enjoyed my time at

Loreto College in Hulme, and each time I pass there now, I always get a little flashback of our time there.

I often find I am thinking outside of the box and have always been brilliant at finding solutions to problems. I think big, and I am always daydreaming. Often, I know what I want to say but don't know how to say it

Dyslexia does not affect intelligence, and research suggests people with the condition are highly creative and intelligent in all they do.

"Out of the struggle, you find that unique gift that comes from your disability."

- Patrick Dempsey, Grey's Anatomy actor

Facing my immigration fears.

When I started studying at Loreto College, I didn't have the right to stay in the UK as my grandma had passed away, and nothing was finalised, so it was up to me. I had no support, and it was hard as I didn't know what to do, as she was the one I depended on to help me. I was confused and didn't know how I would be able to stay. I wasn't settled, as I knew that if I was caught at college without clearance to be in the country, I would be sent back to Jamaica as my main sponsor was no longer alive. Each day I was living in fear, as I didn't want to go back to Jamaica. My heart would miss a beat every time there was a knock on the door, as I was scared that immigration would find and deport me.

I decided that I wasn't going to get married in order to be granted the right to stay in the country. The thought of doing that terrified me, as I wanted to do it for myself without having to depend on someone else. Every day I kept thinking about my situation, and I cried many times about it.

One day I had an idea – a very out-of-the-box idea. I didn't know whether it would work, but I had to take matters into my own hands. I went to the immigration lawyer who had my passport. He was very reluctant to hand it over, but I insisted I wanted it. He was intrigued as to why I wanted it back, but I wasn't forthcoming with the information and just said I wanted my passport. Through my persistence, I got it back and made a start on my idea. I knew writing the letter I planned wouldn't be easy, and a lot was going through my mind. I was scared it wouldn't work, but my thought was that if I didn't try, I wouldn't know, so I got pen and paper and made a start.

It took me quite a few days to complete the letter, but I wrote from my heart and explained my situation. After I finished writing, I went to the post office and sent it by registered mail. After I sent it, I felt relieved and even more scared of it returning with a rejection. I had sleepless nights and really felt alone, as I didn't have anyone to talk to about it, as my grandma was gone.

Almost a week went by, and my worry continued. On the Saturday morning, I was upstairs in my room when I heard the postman. I quickly ran downstairs to get the letters. My heart was pounding as I saw the small brown envelope which had my name on it and was about the size of my passport. I was terrified to open it and was getting hot and sweaty, holding it in my hand. I didn't want to open it, but I knew I had to, so I plucked up the courage, slowly skipping through each page. As I went further in, I saw an embossed stamp which said: "Indefinite leave to remain". I was in shock that I did it. My idea of writing to them worked. I was so happy I cried that whole day as, finally; I was free. I didn't have to look over my shoulder any more or get scared when there was a knock on the door. I didn't have to be scared of going to college or continue to live with the fear of being deported. I was proud that I did all that myself without the help or support of anyone. The joy I felt was second to none, and I am so proud of myself for thinking that I could do it and get the result I wanted.

Key take away

When you get an idea, go for it and see what can happen, as you will never know until you try. The chances are everything will be okay in the end. Don't think that you can't do it. Try, and see, as you are more than capable of taking on any official organisation and getting the required result. Know your worth, and don't be scared to go for it. If you don't ask, you don't get.

My challenges

in the workplace.

"Problem-solving, overcoming and persistence are skills dyslexic people propagate throughout life. The out-of-the-box thinking allows people with dyslexia to thrive, building resilience, positive mindset and knowing they can weather practically anything."

-Lois Letchford, fellow dyslexic, author of the book Reversed.

In my role working for a local government organisation, I got the opportunity to travel all over England, Scotland and Wales, which allowed me to meet people from all walks of life. Being someone who loves to connect with people, I really enjoyed this part of my role; however, having undiagnosed dyslexia in the workplace brought many challenges for me on a daily basis. I wish someone had noticed it during the 17 years I spent working in the corporate world. Despite the challenges that I was facing, I excelled in several areas of my role. My problem-solving skills, empathy for others, my ability to network and find solutions shone through in several areas. I was that go-to person in the office that would negotiate the best deal when finding a venue.

Not remembering things in my job and normal everyday tasks such as making appointments or following instructions were big challenges in my work life. I made simple mistakes, especially when dealing with multiple tasks. My brain goes a thousand miles an hour, and I never stop thinking about all the things I want to do. My thinking is never in a logical order – with no attention span.

Key take away

"We are here for a reason. I believe a bit of the reason is to throw little torches out to lead people through the dark." Whoopi Goldberg

The Dyslexic Mom.

I really feel I didn't help my daughter in her schooling as other parents were able to. She didn't like maths, like me, and I was worried this was something she got from me.

I remember getting frustrated with her and myself, as I felt useless because I couldn't help with her maths homework. She is highly creative. However, when it came to maths, it was like the blind leading the blind. Her algebra homework was the worst. I still don't know the value of x and y. It didn't make any sense to her or to me, like mother, like daughter.

At times I felt lost and would often worry about her abilities in school, and my fears were confirmed when she started to struggle. She loved English and all her other subjects, especially art. She definitely has a great creative side to her.

I remember the parents' evening when they told me my own daughter was struggling with maths. I wish I knew what it was then, as I would have been able to identify why she was struggling so much. However, I didn't even know what it was then, as I had no idea about dyslexia or dyspraxia, so it was difficult for me to ask the school to provide extra support. I was always scared when she had to do projects for school or when she asked for help with her schoolwork as I didn't understand any of it, so I couldn't help her. Oh yes, the dreaded decorating of the Easter bonnet and the egg, with an aim to win, got to me every year as I felt useless. Her egg and bonnet never stood up to much, and she didn't win on any occasion. It was something that was always last-minute as I would feel overwhelmed, so I would keep on putting it off. Then I would often lose track of time and underestimate how long it would take to complete it. I hated the disappointment on her face each year.

It wasn't a nice feeling, and I felt like I was failing her with her education as a mother. It was frustrating because I should have been able to help my daughter do her homework. I wish I knew why I couldn't. I felt lost and inadequate. All these feelings made me feel low, and I was filled with fear at the thought of letting her down. I felt that if she didn't do well in school, I was the one to be blamed.

I was so worried she would struggle to do well in her SATs, and I knew she was worried too, but I didn't know how to help. Not knowing what was holding us back was the worst feeling ever. For each test she had, I reassured her to just do her best and that it didn't matter if she didn't pass. But, deep down, I knew I would have felt a sense of disappointment for both of us because every parent wants their children to do well and not just ok.

Key take away

Don't be too hard on your children. Test results don't define their ability. There are other skills they possess that need nurturing. My daughter is highly creative. She loved art, and singing was her thing at the time. She used to put her all into singing and even won the Ashbury Meadow Got Talent competition when she sang her favourite song. I was there to support her, and I can never forget how proud she was to have won it. The smile on her face said it all. That gave her a great confidence boost, as she had never won anything before.

Pay close attention to your children's education and get to know what subjects they like and don't like. If they don't like a particular subject, find out why. Not liking a specific subject may be an indication they are struggling. Encourage them to focus on their strengths and not waste time on the things that they are not so good at doing.

Learning to drive

around and around the roundabouts.

Learning to drive was one of my biggest challenges. It took me ages and a few attempts. My journey of learning to drive started with Shelton. Like many others in Manchester, we all learnt to drive with him. He was a great instructor with a lot of patience, which is something I needed as I made so many mistakes and misjudgements of space.

I couldn't get my head around directions, and I struggled with knowing my left from my right. Roundabouts were my most hated thing; I would get the sweats as I approached them. I remember taking several driving lessons and spending a lot of money and stopping and starting each time – I wasn't consistent with it. I felt like I really wasn't going to pass my test because I found it draining trying to keep up with so many instructions. My brain wasn't quick to take in the instructions, and I needed to be told over and over again. Within a few minutes of him telling me what to do, I would forget. The angry stares from other drivers made it even worse, and I panicked more. My confidence would be at an all-time low after a driving lesson. I did upset others on the road, and to avoid their anger, I would stare firmly ahead, avoiding any eye contact. My instructor would look at them and nod in an apologetic manner. He spent a lot of time correcting my mistakes, but I was determined to learn. He just kept stepping on the brakes to stop me from crashing.

I didn't ever think I would pass my driving test. I had to take the theory test a few times, too and really had to study hard for it, as I struggled to remember the different road signs and especially the questions that had numbers I needed to remember. After failing over and over again, I didn't give up; I persevered until I passed.

The day I passed my driving test, I hugged the driving instructor and said to her it was like winning the lottery. She turned to me and asked if I had won the lottery before. I told her I hadn't, but it felt like that. She found it hilarious. It was such a great feeling to finally pass it, and it was another reminder not to give up on that dream and that, with perseverance, it can happen.

I do think I would have passed my driving if I had known I had dyslexia and dyspraxia. I really think there should be driving instructors that know the challenges we face and know how to adapt their teaching styles to help people that are dyslexic or dyspraxic.

Key Take away

Never give up on anything you want to achieve. Without knowing it, you are inspiring others with your actions and determination. People will always remember you for the way you have continued to move forward, regardless. Never compare your abilities with others, as they may not possess half the skills and gifts with which you are blessed.

The Dream Job That Became the Nightmare!

2004 was the year I got my dream job, or so I thought. When I came to the UK in 1992, I often told my aunt that I wanted to be a secretary, and that was what I got. The job had everything, but it came with its own trials as an undiagnosed dyslexic. I loved my job at the college, so when I lost it, things weren't easy. I was terrified of starting over again, but finding another job was something I had to do. Even the thought of the application process was very daunting. When I saw this job advertised, I had a feeling I would get it, but I knew I had to make a particularly good application, which frightened me. Dyslexics get overwhelmed with paperwork and deadlines, which leads to procrastination. I kept putting it off, but I knew it had to be done and only I could do it.

I completed the application form and returned it just before the deadline. Oh yes, the overwhelming feeling of completing it had me doing it at the last minute, as usual. I wasn't the best at making applications, so as always, I took a while to complete it. I really took my time and got my friend Jade to check it. I had the instinct to get it checked before I sent it off, as I knew it may have mistakes lurking somewhere in the writing. I got a response from my application about a week after sending it off. I was happy, really happy, and could not wait to share the news with Jade. The letter invited me for an interview, and straight away, I started to prepare. I made sure I noted who was going to interview me, the time and the location. To help me get there on time and to know exactly where I was going, I did a dummy run, visiting the office block before the day of the interview.

I was no longer living in Whalley Range but was further away from Old Trafford. I knew it would take me longer and that I had to plan my time so that I was organised, which wasn't easy. It really wouldn't look good to turn up late for an interview, but we dyslexics often lose track of time and underestimate the time it takes to do things, and getting lost is an everyday challenge. Planning and estimating things were never my strong point. Forgetting details is a regular thing for me, and I was always worried that one day I would forget to collect my daughter from a party or even from school. Luckily, it didn't happen, but I did wonder how future children would fare. If I got this job, I would need to really plan my mornings, so I'd have enough time to catch the two buses I needed to get each morning to work. I had to drop Dellea off at nursery and get to work on time, and that was going to be a mission. I got flustered just by thinking about missing the bus each morning, and every morning was a dash as I was always running late. My concept of time is non-existent. It was like a military mission to get to nursery so that I could get the bus on time to Piccadilly and, from there, to Old Trafford every day, come rain or shine. More than often, it was raining, as this part of the world is known for its rain!

I have a thing about crossing roads. I hated crossing roads, especially if there was traffic coming from all directions. Every morning, I had the sweats crossing Ashton Old Road to get to the nursery. I hated crossing the road then, and I still do now. Some mornings I had to do it with a screaming baby. At first, she hated nursery and cried most days. It broke my heart each morning to leave her screaming, but it was something I had to do to provide for both of us.

Her nursery fees were £600 each month. We had to make do, as that was the only income as a single mom. Travelling on the buses each morning wasn't always a pleasant experience, as I have one of those faces that say come and talk to me; I always get people coming up to me wanting to talk and, because of my empathy for others, I always feel I have to talk to them. You get so many different characters on the bus, from ignorant passengers to grumpy bus drivers who look like they haven't smiled in months. The wet mornings were unbearable, especially in the cold winter months when it snowed.

The interview was great. It went well. I was interviewed by a lovely lady called Wilda. She was lovely, and we really connected, as we both had a Jamaican connection. The chief executive also interviewed me. The day I went for the interview was the same day I had the call telling me I had been successful. I was so happy; I couldn't believe I had gotten the job.

I loved working in Old Trafford, just opposite the cricket club and not far from Manchester United's football ground. Wilda really looked after me, and she was a great manager. But, when someone else took over the management of the team, things started to change. Wilda had a lot of patience; she looked after her team and was very laid back. She was immensely helpful, and when she left, I felt lost. She never made a fuss when I made mistakes in my work.

Every day was a struggle, from the day I started until the day I left. I felt that I couldn't do anything right and like my work was constantly under the spotlight, being scrutinised. I was great at everything else, but not numbers and following procedures.

I had serious imposter syndrome and didn't feel like I belonged. I had no confidence in my abilities, and the struggles just got worse. I would often compare myself and my work with others in the team. I couldn't understand how they did things so effortlessly, while it would take me forever and more!

Key take away

Know your value and your worth in all you do and learn not to compare yourself with others.

Memory and Names.

Like most dyslexics, remembering names has always been a thing that often embarrasses me, as I get names wrong. It can be a big thing for dyslexic individuals. I remember faces, but remembering and pronouncing names is a big no-no. My children get the brunt of it every day, as I call each of their names before getting to the right one. I remember interviewing the lovely Ni-Cola, but I kept calling her Nicole. It's something that happens all the time, but being able to laugh at myself helps a lot. No one is perfect, and in life, you can't take yourself too seriously.

Teachers and Dyslexics.

One of my greatest wishes is for teachers to become more aware of the difficulties people with dyslexia go through. It is always a joy when you meet a teacher who is dyslexic because they understand the issues and know how to empathise. They have the patience to explain things in the simplest way to ensure what they are saying is understood.

What Can Teachers Do to Help Dyslexics in Their Classrooms?

- Test students orally rather than in writing

- Give students additional time on tests and be patient about their speed.

- Don't judge their intelligence and knowledge using spelling tests.

- Allow students to dictate their work.

- Reduce their homework and be lenient with their grades when marking.

- Don't assess their work based on their handwriting and spelling, as dyslexics are not always good at spelling or have the best handwriting.

- Don't give students tasks which involve copying from a board.

- Don't ask students to read aloud in front of the whole class.

- Give task instructions slowly and ensure that students have a full understanding of what is required of them

- Provide students with a structure for written tasks.

- Monitor their progress and give constant encouragement.

- Praise their effort and celebrate their achievements.

Don't Let Anything Stop You – Studying.

Benjamin Franklin said: "Tell me and I forget, teach me and I remember, involve me and I learn."

No one else can fulfil your purpose, but you can develop a strong belief that anything is possible, and you are greater than you think.

When you are gifted, nothing can stop you, and that is something that needs to be nurtured. People that are dyslexic, or those that don't even know they have a learning difference, can feel they are not intelligent enough to go on to further education. Sadly, many young people leave the education system due to frustration and feelings of inadequacy. I was one of them, and when I left college, going to university wasn't something I felt I could do. I didn't feel I was clever enough to achieve a degree.

"Dyslexic thinking has changed the world with the arts, technology, design and beyond. Having dyslexia brings about a way of viewing life in unique ways. Dyslexic thinkers bring something unique to the party that is humanity, and their strengths should be cherished, and their weaknesses supported."
-John Hicks, The Studying with Dyslexia Blog and Parenting Dyslexia

The struggles are very real if you have dyslexia and are studying. I am pretty sure the things I experienced, others have too. I was always curious as to why it took me so long to simply copy from the board. I would look around, and everyone had finished. Because I felt embarrassed, I would tell the lecturer to go ahead, even when I wasn't finished – I didn't want to slow down the rest of the class.

This was all before I got the support I needed, and as I have mentioned in other parts of this book, early diagnosis is key in order to access the support and assistive technology available to dyslexic students. Yes, the support will help massively and can assist in making the journey less stressful and challenging in many ways. With my short-term memory issues, I couldn't remember information for any length of time. I would read a journal article one day but don't ask me what it was about the next day. My study style is different, as it will take me longer to understand the information, and I have found the combination of dyslexia and dyspraxia is a double deficit that affects my social and academic life.

"You don't need to be a top student in school to be the top in your career."

-Will Wheeler, founder/director at Neurodiversity Academy, author and motivational speaker

I can't believe

you are Dyslexic.

"I realised my dyslexia was my gift. As much as I didn't fit into the standard, I ran with it. It was empowering."

- Erin Brockovich

I have always been a fast thinker and very solution-driven; finding solutions to problems is one of my greatest strengths. If there is a problem, I am always able to find the solution, and I am enormously proud of this strength. My great dyslexic strengths often make it hard for people to believe I have dyslexia, which is due to their lack of understanding that dyslexia has nothing to do with your level of intelligence or your ability to do things.

Individuals with dyslexia don't walk around with a sticker saying they are dyslexic. I couldn't do that even if I wanted to, as I didn't know what was affecting me and the way I did things.

I felt great delight when I found out Will Smith was also dyslexic; that really did bring me closer to him. Well, I wish! I have always been a big fan, and growing up, I watched most, if not all, *The Fresh Prince of Bel-Air* episodes and even enjoyed 'Boom! Shake the Room,' which was one of his most well-known tracks back in my young days.

I was really shocked but happy at the same time. I mean, this guy has been one of my favourite actors, along with Idris Elba, of course. I never knew that Will Smith was part of our special club, along with others, such as some of the world's most famous people: Albert Einstein, Thomas Eddison, Henry Ford, British film director Steve McQueen, Richard Branson, Prince Harry, Princess Beatrice, Victoria Beckham, Jay Blades MBE, The Wright Brothers who are responsible for the great invention of aeroplanes, and many others. Individuals with dyslexia are simply amazing, with so much to offer the world. We are not going to change for anyone, as it's our uniqueness of who we are and what we can do. I feel honoured to be part of the great percentage of people that are dyslexic.

So many other successful people and celebrities are dyslexic, and I recently came across Mollie King, former The Saturday's singer, who shared her experience in a powerful speech at an all-party parliamentary group as an ambassador for the British Dyslexia Association (BDA).

Talking about her experience, she said: "The key is being diagnosed as early as possible. It breaks my heart that there could be people out there struggling through life unnecessarily because they've not been diagnosed and are still feeling stupid the way I did." She said she spent her childhood feeling "stupid" before being diagnosed with dyslexia. She reminded people that dyslexia "isn't something that defeats you" and it doesn't mean you can't reach your full potential.

Case Study One

The Word" by Heather Christian

I am honoured to have been asked by my beautiful, intelligent, courageous, strong, and graceful friend to contribute to this fine book. Without further ado, here goes.

Whether you know me in person, through a friend, vaguely or as a total stranger, I am a Jamaican Canadian philanthropist and founder of the Jamaica Dyslexia Association (JDA). I am an author of the JDA Handbook and the mother of an amazing adult son who, as a child, frequently said to me, "Reading is fundamental." The biggest thing I want you to know about me is that I am a proud dyslexic.

In the grand scheme of it, this is a small part of my dyslexia story. I heard the word "dyslexia" for the first time at the age of 14 as a volunteer at the senior's centre. I was working with one of the clients, a retired schoolteacher, on the monthly activities list when she asked if I had dyslexia because of how I wrote and spelt. Ever since I have become fixated with the word.

My struggles with dyslexia led me through frustration, trepidation and distress. It's a personal goal of mine to unlock dyslexia in Jamaica. Hence my brainchild, the JDA, was established in 2016. It is the first and only charitable organisation in Jamaica that focuses one hundred per cent on dyslexia. The JDA's vision is to be an effective advocate that influences public policy and laws by enlightening government officials, educational institutions, employers and the public on the needs of those who have dyslexia. The mission of the JDA is to be the leading provider of services to people who have dyslexia, to help them reach their highest personal, educational and financial growth to benefit themselves and society.

Growing up in Clarendon, Jamaica, during the early 1960s, no one in my community understood the meaning of dyslexia. My parents had no idea that I had a learning disability. In infant school (preschool), I clearly remember having issues learning the simplest of things. My favourite aunt, who everyone called Teacher, was also my classroom teacher. She tried helping me understand the alphabet, but I had such difficulties adapting. I wanted to learn how to make choices for myself and feel good about the choices I made. I spent most of my time drawing things instead of learning the alphabet. My aunt never got angry at me; instead, she encouraged my vivid imagination. Yet, I often thought that I disappointed her because I was not as bright as the other children. My aunt passed away when I was six years old, and that was when school was no longer fun for me.

In primary school, I struggled in silence from the outset. Being unable to comprehend 'left' and 'right' and finding it hard to remember sequences was challenging. I disliked reading aloud because I sometimes mispronounced the words. My handwriting was very messy, and I set letters and figures the wrong way. When sitting down to take a test, the panic would build, and my anxieties led to many nightmares. My worst years in primary school were from grades 1 to 3. I felt like a complete failure. To help me get through the days, I would let my continually active imagination take me to places where books have no words, only colourful imagery. At the end of grade 3, I failed so badly that I dreaded for sure the principal would ask my parents not to send me back to school because I was not learning.

To my surprise, I got placed in grade 4B. The new teacher, Miss Mullings, had a gift. Throughout the year, she gave me some relief from my educational nightmares. She told me I was wise beyond my years. I felt inadequate as a good student until I was placed at the top of my class at the end of the year. She even selected me to deliver an end-of-term thank you speech to one of our other teachers who was leaving. On the day of the event, I rippled with excitement. When called upon, I walked proudly to the podium, standing tall, neatly put together in my new blue uniform, with a big blue ribbon in my hair, and to complete it, a new pair of shiny black shoes with blue socks. I took a bow with a big smile on my face. I thought that I could do it because I had read my speech a million times the night before. I began my speech with these words, "On behalf of the teachers and students of this block ..." Suddenly, I became mute. I could not remember the rest of my speech. It was my first public awkwardness and a big blow to my self-esteem. Again, I felt that I had let my teacher down. The following year, they let me skip grades five and six (a big mistake). I started secondary school in grade 7B with children who were a few years older than me.

I completed my high school years in Canada, where the nightmares got worse. The culture shock intensified my anxiety. In school, taking notes was frustrating. I had become accustomed to permanent migraines just from looking at the black/whiteboard. Sadly, what frustrated me most was when I composed a sentence in my head and then wrote it down, I could not recognise my poor comprehension. Most of what I learnt had to be by listening. I have compensated for my learning difficulties by creating unorthodox ways to get around them. The only positive experience I had in high school was in visual arts. I received excellent grades, and the teacher always displayed my artwork. Surprisingly, I went on to graduate from college with honours. Having this distinction on my college transcript was a big deal and a boost to my self-confidence.

I was tested for dyslexia when I was in university. The educational psychologist who diagnosed me said I got by in school because I developed a unique skill for solving problems and tackling challenges by creating coping strategies.

After my diagnosis, the university provided me with a note-taker and recording devices for my class lectures. In the '70s and 'eighties, most students didn't even own a personal computer. Eventually, I got one by the time I entered my second year in the early 'nineties. Owning a home computer with a word processor assisting with spell checks was terrific. It helped with the development of my writing. I was able to turn in my assignments on time in a neat and tidy fashion. Indeed, I benefitted tremendously from using assistive technology tools to further my education and gain meaningful employment.

Since my diagnosis, I wear dyslexia like a badge of honour. To paraphrase award-winning film director Steven Spielberg, who is also dyslexic, "It was like finding the missing piece of an unfinished puzzle." To this day, I'm a little bashful when people seem surprised to find out I have dyslexia. Some would ask, "How can you have a degree, be an education administrator, a writer, a director on so many boards and yet be dyslexic?" But, in all of this, the advantages of having dyslexia outweigh the struggles.

Thanks to my aunt, my first teacher, who gave me the courage to use my imagination. Miss Mullings, my grade 4 teacher, saw beyond my learning difficulties, and my first-year university professor encouraged me to do more writing. I succeeded as a student and professional because I learnt to value myself and build a strong work ethic with a realistic sense of my abilities and competence. Furthermore, I was extremely fortunate to be in Canada, where access to dyslexic accommodations was readily available.

Dyslexia doesn't just affect people's learning: it impacts their everyday lives. Therefore, awareness, understanding, early identification and assessment for dyslexia are critical. I believe that dyslexia is a learning difference that can become a disability when you don't know you have it.

Schools and what they need to know.

"All students should get reading instruction that is intensive, explicit, supportive and fun."

-Tiffany James, Nessy Learning

The English language is not easy to understand, and still today, I laugh at myself at how certain words always trip me up when I try to pronounce them. I often get confused with words such as 'their' and 'there', 'threw' and 'true', 'here' and 'hear', plus several others.

Schools play a significant part in your life. Children spend most of their young days there. I wish they had more understanding of how to spot the possible struggles children have. It is vital any issues are identified early so the correct support can be put into place. Imagine struggling in silence, but no one understands why. Having the right support from the start can really contribute to performance.

My school life wasn't a happy one because I struggled in silence through basic school, as they call it in Jamaica, and the school I went to for two years after I came to the UK. When I started school in England, I had no idea that all the things I was struggling with had a name. I mean, in the nineties, the word dyslexia wasn't a word I would have associated with myself as it wasn't a popular word in my community or environment. Few people understood what it was or even that they themselves could possibly have it. All the way through my school years, I felt stupid, so I would often compare myself with others and what they were able to do. I felt useless most of the time and didn't understand why certain things were so difficult for me to do, especially when I was so good at other things.

Labels, Labels and more labels

"I carried around a lot of negative labels that were given to me growing up when I didn't have a diagnosis, so when I was finally diagnosed, I understood why things were such a struggle growing up."

-Keisha Adair Swaby

Believing the negative things and false labels we have been lumbered with from an incredibly early age can affect us more than we know. You name it, and we have been called it. As they say, it's none of your business what others think of you; however, sometimes it's hard to not take things personally, especially when it's about your personality. To be honest, I have been vulnerable, as it took me an awfully long time to realise other people's opinions and what they think of me are not my problem. I hated myself at times and the way I was, and yes, there were times when I felt stupid and really believed what others thought about me.

I have never said I am perfect – far from it

"After years of feeling like dyslexia is some sort of deficit, I discovered how wrong I was. Yes, maybe some things are a little tricky, but this can be overcome with the right learning inputs. Dyslexia is a huge benefit. Having a brain that thinks differently, is more creative and can handle multiple things at once makes for one powerhouse, once you lose the negative things you perceive. Yes, dyslexia makes you different, but 'different' is an advantage!"

-Matthew Head, senior vehicle design engineer at RML Group/founder of Dyslexia Hacks, fellow dyslexic

People that don't know much about dyslexia and dyspraxia will never understand what we go through. Please don't think for one minute that it was easy for me to write this book, as I had my own challenges that many don't see. It took me a lot of time and writer's block along the way. I doubted myself as to whether I could finally complete it. I remember speaking to my publisher, Marcia and Yanique, about my deadline and how I just needed to stop writing and send the manuscript. I wanted to carry on writing because I can be overly critical about my work, and I didn't feel I was at the stage where I could send it off. This book has been a labour of love, and I wanted to make sure I did my best writing it and that I gave it my all.

The challenges
people don't see.

There are so many little things we do that show what we go through, like doing a simple post on social media. Sometimes, no matter how much I check for errors, they are still there, but I can't see them. I remember posting a quote I had created in my Empowering Dyslexics group and totally missed a word out even though I had checked it several times. I had to laugh when my friend, who is also dyslexic, messaged me to ask if I noticed I had missed out a word. I had to quickly change it. However, it was the same post that I had used on LinkedIn and Instagram, so I had to quickly amend them all and repost them.

My phone always tells the story about my dyspraxia and how many times I have dropped it. The screen is cracked from dropping it several times a day. Yes, I do know that people drop their phones, but believe me, my phone has been dropped a lot more times because of my lack of coordination.

There are certain things I do, and I guess the same happens to other dyslexics, too, such as forgetting to reply to messages, not remembering dates, birthdays, appointments, events, and names. The list goes on. I am forever calling people the wrong name, which can be embarrassing. I really do apologise. If you are reading this and I have ever called you the wrong name, please just correct me rather than staring at me blankly. I have been in so many situations where this has left me wondering why the person would suddenly switch off from our conversation, and later on, I would realise I had called them the wrong name. We really don't intend to do these things on purpose; they just happen because of the way we think. All we need is a bit of understanding, so don't judge us, just be patient.

Despite our challenges, some of the greatest inventors, businesspeople, musicians, film directors, designers and extraordinary sportspeople are dyslexic. We are able to fly today because of the Wright brothers, who were brave enough to invent the aeroplane. Richard Branson is a great businessperson in his own right and has created multiple businesses with services we use on a daily basis. We have all enjoyed wonderful music from great musicians such as Ed

Sheeran, Paul McCartney, John Lennon and Gwen Stefani, to name but a few. I am a big fan of Sir Steve McQueen, CBE, and I am so proud of all his achievements as an award-winning Black film producer, screenwriter and director, who has brought us some great shows, such as the *Small Axe* series and the film *12 Years a Slave*, to name but a few. Whoopi Goldberg is a great Black actor who is dyslexic. I have always admired her great acting ever since her role in the classic 1985 film, *The Color Purple*, plus many others. Growing up, I was and still am a big fan of Will Smith and Usher, so when I found out they, too, were dyslexic, I realised our skills and talents exist in every industry.

There are so many others within our communities who are doing great things every day. For those individuals I haven't already mentioned, just know that I salute you and your contribution to this world.

Don't Give Up
on That Dream.

After discovering Les Brown in 2013, I had a burning desire to work with him one day, and that dream came true in June 2020 when I got the opportunity to join the Les Brown Power Voice Program. On the course, I met some amazing people, and I was honoured to be mentored by one of the world's best motivational speakers. He is also dyslexic and was written off in school by his teachers, but he has gone on to help millions of people worldwide realise their dreams. *"Dyslexia is my superpower. I am forever grateful for these abilities and would feel depleted if there was ever a day that I became 'normal.' Dyslexia is so much a part of me, I find it difficult to separate the two."* Raheem (Rodney L. Grant) Mu Khepera, MBE, founder at Prime Unltd (fellow dyslexic)

I remember doing a podcast with Nigel Beckles. My friend and fellow dyslexic, Jannette Barrett, sent me a message saying I made her laugh from a line in the interview about my fascination and obsession with the radio. I shared my childhood story of my dream to work on the radio. I was totally obsessed with it and how someone could be inside talking, and I couldn't see them. I had a dream that one day I would be that voice on the radio and told myself it would happen.

Everything changed in 2016 after leaving my job. I started my foundation degree at Manchester College. One day while on campus, I received an email from the student engagement officer, Jenny, about a project at BBC Radio Manchester. Straightaway, I knew how great it would be to do a project with such a well-known station.

I was so excited to read about how great this project would be, and straightaway, I knew I wanted to go for it, but like always, I was dreading all that I would have to do to apply, as the application needed a lot of information. It all seemed to be so overwhelming, and the amount of information I had to write about myself meant I left it to the last minute and nearly missed the deadline. I didn't complete the application all at once as I found it really overwhelming. However, I eventually completed it and sent it off. I thought I would never hear anything back; after all, it was the BBC. Why would they want me, the girl that used to break the radio? I was suffering from imposter syndrome in a big way and didn't believe that I was good enough to do it.

Over a month passed, and I didn't hear anything back until, one day, I sat in my lecture and received a call from a private number. I didn't want to answer it in the classroom in front of everyone, so I left the lecture and went in the corridor, and I am so glad that I did because it was the start of another dream coming true. I was so excited and scared at the same time and worried about the whole process, as there were several stages of the interview process, I had to go through to be part of the project. I made it through all the stages and got to be part of the Over to You Project. As part of it, I got to produce a show for Mike Sweeney, which was fun, as he is hilarious. The whole process was amazing, and I gained a lot of experience and met some great people, some of whom I am still in contact with today. The celebration at the end was even more rewarding, with a brilliant event held at Manchester Town Hall with other well-known television and radio presenters.

At the end of the project, I realised the impact of radio and how much I enjoyed doing it.

Helping Others to See Their Gift.

"Dyslexia is not a disease nor a liability It's a different view to the world."

-Alex Onalaja Jr, entrepreneur, author, speaker, mentor (fellow Dyslexic)

I have a passion for helping others, as I have needed help myself, so I know that others need my help too. I have lived it, and you can't beat the lived experience of anyone. As my value for help goes a long way, I want to help others that may be going through exactly what I have been through. The great Les Brown said your story will become the blueprint for someone else going through what you have been through. I created Empowering Dyslexics to be that source of empowerment for so many. Not everyone is dyslexic, but even if they are not dyslexic themselves, I bet they know someone who is. Support and understanding are a big deal to dyslexics, so we need that support to get on with what we need to do, and we need understanding of our challenges so that we can outsource things that are not our strong points.

My vision for Empowering Dyslexics is massive in every sense. I want all dyslexics and everyone to know they are here for a purpose, and they just need to find what they are passionate about and focus on that.

Why I am blessed with dyslexia

"I was born with something that makes me see things differently. It makes me never want to give up. It makes me refuse to settle for average. It's dyslexia and I am glad I have it."

- Benjamin James Kershaw, CEO of Golden Egg Group

As a dyslexic, I am naturally drawn to other dyslexics, and the quote above is from another fellow dyslexic. We connected because we had that in common.

My unseen challenges

There are several things I do that make me laugh at myself on a daily basis, like the time I was driving and thought I had lost my phone, only to realise I was using it as a satnav. It was such a horrible feeling as I was mortified that I had lost my phone.

When people see my posts on social media, they don't know how many times I have edited that one post, and even after checking and rechecking, I post it and then spot a mistake. I would have to edit it over and over again just to get it right. I once posted 'going love now' instead of 'going live now'! Even on my radio show, I remember doing an interview and forgetting to put my mic on throughout the whole interview, which meant that no one could hear me asking the guest any of the questions. Double and triple booking myself is another thing I do very often, so now I have to use the calendar on my phone to book my meetings and events. Forgetting other people's names and not being able to spell them is another big challenge, as I hate getting other people's names wrong. When I make mistakes, I try not to be too hard on myself as this could lead to feelings of uselessness, and I know that I am not useless and that everyone makes mistakes and have challenges in their life.

Many things I do, I am sure other dyslexics experience every day too. I am always getting into trouble for not responding to messages or emails.

I remember scheduling my radio show, and one week in March, it was also International Women's

Day, and I totally forgot, so I didn't schedule any women on my show on that weekend.

Sometimes people may think I am ignoring them, but that's not the case. I will see the message, then leave it with the intention of getting back to it, and then forget to reply. It is never intentional, just missed messages, as I call them. I can tell you that I have burnt many pots in my kitchen because of forgetfulness. On one occasion, I left the pot on the cooker, and it was only when I almost reached my destination that I remembered that I had left it on the cooker. Trust me, that was scary.

Case Study Two

"Out of the Darkness" by Vanessa Peat

Prior to my diagnosis, it was like being in a dark tunnel navigating my own way. The journey was incredibly scary as there were so many unknowns. However, I learnt to navigate. Not in the conventional way, feeling blind; I navigated my path by feeling the different textures upon my unsteady feet. Sometimes the ground was steep and uphill, making me stumble and fall. Other times it was flat, and I was getting somewhere. However, the path remained uncomfortable, as I did not know where I was travelling to. Sometimes I felt stuck in muddy puddles, which meant I felt trapped. Other times I saw a glimmer of the puddles ahead of me, and with time, I managed to dodge some of those. While on this journey, the isolation remained, even though I could hear others. They sounded like their journey was such fun; I longed to be part of their togetherness. But it was not my time.

Then one day, out of the blue, someone turned a light on. It was such a shock. Although joyous, as I could now see, it was frightening as there was so much to take in. Little by little, step by step, with good counsel and support, I began to understand me, one step at a time. Initially, I was diagnosed with dyslexia and later with dyspraxia with visual stress. Understanding this part of me helped me complete a puzzle. It gave me deep clarity and insight about how I must best learn and work for me to succeed.

This has challenged me on so many levels, Psychologically and emotionally; this has sometimes been a heavy load to carry. However, I would never change the gifts I have been granted, which are unique to me. I am now an individual who is determined and persevering in the face of adversity, an individual determined to face every obstacle with courage, knowing it may take me longer and require so much more effort and resilience to reach my goal.

One of the greatest lessons I have learnt is to surround myself with those individuals who love and care for me, who will cheer me on in my hardest and most challenging moments and give me the courage to persevere. Like many journeys through tunnels, there is more often than not a light at the end!

Dyslexia Awareness
Empowering Everyone.

Empowering parents
How to spot dyslexia.

As much as I wish I had been diagnosed in my childhood, it wasn't something that was possible for me growing up in Jamaica. I had no chance of my parents knowing that I had a learning difference. They certainly didn't know anything about dyslexia or dyspraxia, let alone getting any early support. I am from the rural part of Jamaica, so dyslexia was unheard of at the time, and even today, many parents there still don't know anything about it and what to look for in their own children.

Every child is different and will develop at different stages; however, there are things that parents need to look out for, such as their child's speech development, reading and writing skills, their engagement in certain subjects, as they will excel in the subjects they love. Dyslexics are known to be highly creative in what they do, so they are directed by their passion and what they enjoy doing. Their strengths always shine through, and once these strengths are discovered, nurtured and supported, that child will be unstoppable in all that they dream of achieving.

Empowering dyslexics in the workplace.

"Us dyslexic people, we've got it going on. We are the architects. We are the designers."

-Benjamin Zephaniah

While working, I encountered many challenges because of my undiagnosed dyslexia. My experience in the corporate world wasn't a good one, as I really struggled with many elements of my role. Not knowing meant that, throughout my seventeen years of working in an office environment, I suffered from severe anxiety. I always left tasks until the last minute because I struggled to prioritise my workload. I was constantly overwhelmed by information overload.

However, while I was struggling in silence, I excelled in many other ways, such as my people skills, as I am a great communicator, so I am particularly good at negotiating and networking, with a passion for finding solutions to problems. One of my roles within the team was event administration, so while away attending events, I excelled at helping the delegates, so if they had an issue, I would be the one to find a solution. I loved networking and was known for my customer service skills and can-do attitude. Taking minutes in meetings gave me the greatest anxiety, and the task of understanding and remembering what was said was even worse.

I really wish I had been diagnosed earlier, as it would have prevented the struggles I encountered in the workplace. Looking back at my time in the corporate world, I missed reaching my full potential because I didn't have a diagnosis.

The key is having a formal diagnosis to get the support needed, as it's a legal requirement for employers to provide the appropriate support and adjustments to their dyslexic employees. Employers need to learn more about these learning differences and embrace them because once they are identified, employers can provide their employees with a supportive environment, which will lead to a better understanding from their employer and work colleagues. Employers should always pay attention to employees that struggle with certain aspects of their job, for example:

- Taking longer to complete simple tasks.

- Spelling difficulties.

- Difficulty in prioritising tasks and meeting deadlines.

- Task avoidance.

- Procrastination.

- Lack of time management.

- Lack of interest in complex tasks.

- Difficulty retaining information (poor short-term memory).

- Lack of structure and organising workload.

Due to stigma and embarrassment, not every employee will feel comfortable disclosing that they have a learning difference. Some of the biggest challenges I faced in the workplace were information overload, organising my work, time management and career progression. Processes and procedures such as interviews and tests can cause anxiety for many dyslexic individuals. Exams, tests and interviews are not the best way to highlight our skills and intelligence. When faced with these tasks, it takes us longer to complete them because we need to get a full understanding of what we need to do. We need to work out a plan of how to complete them, which then takes up more time, and as we know, time tends to go fast when in those situations.

Employers need to change their perception of dyslexia and the way they do things. It's good for them to remember that not everyone is the same and one size doesn't fit all. Keep it simple, and don't miss out on recruiting some of the most amazing people due to a lack of understanding. Focus on the dyslexic strengths, not the challenges. Any workplace will benefit from employing people with dyslexia because of their ability to communicate, see the bigger picture and explore, to name but a few.

Empowering employers to help their employees.

"My dyslexia is not a disability, but an ability to think differently and if this world needs anything at this moment, it is people who think differently."

-Jo Malone, CBE, British perfumer

Every workplace could benefit from the greatness of dyslexia, and every employer needs to recognise the value of employing and having dyslexics in their workforce because of the great skills they possess. Dyslexics think big and out of the box time and time again – that's what we do. Often, we will also have a million and one things in our heads while trying to understand it all. Understanding is key, and as we do things differently, we also learn differently. I know that, personally, I am a visual learner. If you tell me how to do it, I will struggle, but if you show me how to do it, I will take it in better. You might have to show me a few times, but I know I will understand it eventually.

The big thinking and visionary skills that dyslexics possess help them to look at things differently, so they are exceptionally good at finding solutions to problems in a simplified way.

Personally, I really struggled to complete forms, especially job applications, because I find them overwhelming, and they are often long and tedious.

Tips for employers:

- Get to know each of your employees and learn more about the way they do things, understanding their learning style

- Encourage inclusivity which will help employees to feel comfortable in disclosing their condition

- Observe their strengths and give employees tasks suited to their learning style

- Take note of tasks they avoid and find out why they are finding it difficult

- Make job application forms simple and short

- When presenting information, use bullet points rather than large paragraphs

- When scheduling meetings, ensure they are short and well structured

- When recruiting, use different methods of testing, such as recording information, so they can also listen rather than being overloaded by written information

- When conducting tests as part of interviews, allow extra time

- Don't be critical about their spelling – it's not a strength for many

- Don't criticise their performance or speed when completing tasks

- Dyslexics need encouragement, praise and support – don't ignore their struggles and needs

- Provide consistent support with personal development and performance

"The more that we encourage each other to learn about how to support dyslexics, the better it will be for the world." La Vasia Bullard, instructional coach, Thomasville Heights Elementary School, US

Empowering schools helping future generations.

"Sometimes, the most brilliant and intelligent minds do not shine on standardised tests because they don't have standardised minds."

-Diane Ravitch, Research Professor of Education, New York University

Like many others, my experience of school wasn't enjoyable, and it can be daunting and frustrating for any child, especially those children with learning differences. On the 25th of October 2019, BBC News reported that "Schools are failing to diagnose at least 80% of dyslexic pupils". Therefore, all these children are leaving the education system without a diagnosis. This is a big issue that needs rectifying fast so that future generations don't suffer like many have done already.

The education system needs to pay more attention to the different abilities that exist in their classrooms, as each child learns differently and at a different pace, so knowing their learning style will help to direct how they should be taught. When a child is interested in something, they will really excel at it, as they won't become easily bored. I remember how I struggled in my history lessons in secondary school because I just wasn't interested, as I didn't understand any of it. I loved art but hated history!

I saw a beautiful quote recently which said: "Every child has a different learning style and pace. Each child is unique, not only capable of learning but also capable of succeeding." (Robert John Meehan) This resonated with me because it's so true.

Teachers need to be able to identify the special gifts their students possess from an early age to provide them with the right support from the start. Early diagnosis is key, so the child will grow up understanding that they learn differently, and they are gifted. All teachers should be trained to identify whether a child has traits of a learning difference. Often, teachers and schools are too quick to label a child as a troublemaker because of poor behaviour, which is often a sign that something deeper is going on that is affecting their behaviour. To deflect and cover up what they are going through, they can often be seen as the class clown. Distraction is a common thing, especially when it's hard to engage or focus on something they are not interested in. Most dyslexics are visual learners, meaning they like to learn with a hands-on approach, so show them and ensure they fully understand what they need to do.

"I wish teachers were more aware of the ying and yang with dyslexia. There are some challenges: the written word, spelling, things like that are more difficult for dyslexics. But the imagination, the storytelling, the communication, the empathy, all these positives are sometimes neglected within the school system."

-Dr Maggie Aderin-Pocock, space scientist, fellow dyslexic

What teachers need to do to empower their students

- Find out what subjects students are interested in
- Praise their efforts and don't point out their mistakes in front of the whole class, as this will cause shame and embarrassment
- Be understanding when they are struggling with something and encourage them to see the best in themselves

I know that there are teachers out there making a big difference in their own way, like Mrs Yearsley from Inspire Academy in Ashton, who I met recently at a dyslexia event. I was really impressed with the great work she is doing to support her students with dyslexia on a daily basis. She even has a dedicated Twitter page called @DyslexiaInspire

The dyslexic student

"Inclusion is not bringing people into what already exists, it is making a new space a better space for everyone."

-George Dei, Professor, Ontario Institute for Studies in Education, University of Toronto

My experience of studying will be like others in many ways. From my own experience at university, I wish my dyslexia had been picked up at an earlier age. Finding out that I had severe dyslexia and dyspraxia in the last few weeks of my degree didn't help, and I found many areas of my studies challenging. I really enjoy learning, but things like the speed at which I process information and navigate through information online cause difficulties and anxieties.

While some receive a formal diagnosis at a young age, I have noticed that a large number of people do not receive a diagnosis until they start their university journey. I know so many from the Black community that have also been diagnosed at university. This highlights the issue that so many have slipped through the net and are undiagnosed because they didn't continue their studies towards further or higher education.

Overcoming my own study challenges

"When you commend me for being creative, compassionate, driven, empathetic, insightful, intuitive, you are complimenting me on some of the beautiful qualities that are a result of having dyslexia."
-Monica Ledgister, fellow dyslexic

"The advantages of dyslexia are that my brain puts information in my head in a different way."
-Whoopi Goldberg

Studying comes with many challenges for those with learning differences because of the way we understand and process information. I am not going to say studying is easy, and there are a lot of things that you will go through before you come out on the other side. There are so many emotions to get through: lack of motivation, confusion, confidence, imposter syndrome, and the whole shebang! With assignment after assignment, I would feel excited to get started before that overwhelming feeling would kick in, and I would sit there staring at my laptop while time was ticking away. I wouldn't know where to start, and the vast amount of information I would have to deal with just became too much. This would always leave me feeling frustrated, as I was not getting enough done as I had planned. We daydream a lot and our minds have many tabs open. The intentions are there, but it's difficult to get them from my brain and make them sound good on paper. With information overload, navigating through it all can become tiring and often leads to repeated procrastination. Online studies can be difficult to navigate, and keeping on top of everything can be daunting. Without support, it's hard, but with the right support, you can navigate through it all.

While studying for my master's, our course was switched to online learning, and while the university did all it could to help, I still felt disconnected due to my own learning style. I was swamped with all we had to do each week, and the overwhelming feeling would take over, so I wouldn't engage as much as I should have done. It was really frustrating, and so many times, I nearly missed important sessions. If it wasn't for other students, I would have totally missed them.

Exams are the worst, and like many others, I don't like them because it's not a great way to test people with learning differences. Exams are my living nightmare, and I would love to see a future without exams, especially for dyslexic individuals.

"Challenges give us the opportunity to master the art of complexity and become a genius of solutions of all kinds."

-Merline Ulysse

Empowering

students study tips:

- Get a good understanding of what is required when given a task or an assignment
- Give yourself plenty of time to complete tasks, as we can often misjudge the time it will take to complete
- Don't leave things until the last minute
- Work at a suitable pace to avoid becoming overwhelmed by your workload
- Take regular breaks and do something relaxing
- Be kind to yourself and don't compare your grades with others – they are not you, and you are not them

- Use the resources available such as study skill support and assistive technology to help, and get help from the library
- Connect with other dyslexic individuals for support and be part of a community of people that understand
- Get a study buddy or an accountability partner to avoid procrastination
- Break down each task into bite size pieces
- Set small achievable goals
- Never feel afraid of asking questions to get clarity
- Have faith and believe in your abilities
- Always remember that you can do it, too; just keep going
- Don't be too hard on yourself – be kind
- Celebrate your achievements and reward yourself
- Remember that self-care is key
- Have faith and believe you will get through it. All the hard work will pay off, and you will be glad you never gave up!
- Show appreciation to those that have supported you on your journey

Don't miss the opportunity to graduate; it's such a great feeling on that day, and it is proof that you have done it and that you can do anything, which will give you a confidence boost. It's a great feeling walking across that stage, knowing that you persevered and achieved what at first seemed like the hardest thing ever. Dance across that stage and be proud of how far you have come on your journey. Dyslexia is more common than you think, and with the right support, dyslexic students can achieve all that they want with determination and persistence. At my graduation, I was truly humbled to receive an award and prize for Outstanding Community Spirit. It was totally unexpected, but it made me realise that the work that I have been doing to create change had been noticed.

Dyslexia and procrastination

"A person can waste a lot of years of their life procrastinating. What strategy are you using to overcome procrastination? Don't waste another day as right now someone is in the hospital begging God for the opportunity that you have!"

-Carl Foster, author, fellow dyslexic

I know procrastination is universal behaviour which affects many; however, we dyslexics seem to get a double portion, all day, every day. We make the effort to write the task list, but it will take us a lot longer to get through it. This is a big challenge for us, which is often caused by becoming massively overwhelmed. We will just put it off until we can't anymore, as the deadline is looming just around the corner. When it came to my studying time, I would sit there and stare at the laptop, not knowing where to start. Of course, I have done a mind map and know what I want to say, but the words don't always come. I have a clear idea in my head of what I want to write but getting it on paper sounding right is something else. While procrastination has no benefit to anyone, it's easy to become frustrated with your lack of productivity, so be forgiving to yourself. It's important to get an accountability partner or just someone to check in on your progress when you are working on something. Be gentle with yourself and believe that you will get it done. Don't be afraid to ask for help and make use of assistive technology to help with the process.

Empowering Families.

"Always remember that personal acceptance comes before personal development. Remember that labels are for jars and not for people. Remember that you deserve to be celebrated, not just tolerated! Remember who you are because that person is more than enough."

-Ruth-Ellen Danquah,
neurodiversity consultant, fellow dyslexic

Having family members that understand why you do things the way you do can make all the difference. If there is someone in your family with dyslexia, you might know about it. However, there might be people in your family that are dyslexic but haven't been formally diagnosed. Often, they can go through life just masking their difficulties because they are ashamed and don't know much about it. Dyslexia is hereditary, so it can be passed down through the generations. The chances are, if someone in your family is dyslexic, there will be someone else in the family that is also highly likely to be dyslexic.

Dyslexia is not something that affects just certain parts of society and families. Worldwide, everyone has their own stories and experiences. Something that always made me laugh was when Victoria Beckham said in several interviews: "Dyslexia doesn't run in the family– it gallops." In those articles, she also hinted that all her four children had dyslexia (Robinson, 2019). She is an amazing creative and has showcased her skills as a fashion designer in her own right. The world is full of great people who have dyslexia with extraordinary creative skills that will always be needed in society, and that is a great and positive strength that should be nurtured.

Embarrassment and shame are some of the biggest reasons people don't admit that something isn't quite right. They may find it difficult to pinpoint what it may be. A lack of understanding can lead to confusion.

Empowering strengths

"Every dyslexic person has the feeling there is more in him or her more than others see."

-Norda, dyslexia influencer, fellow dyslexic

There are so many areas in which I would like to see changes and improvements. Other dyslexics can really relate to these challenges.

Empowering genuine inclusion

Being a Black woman comes with its own challenges but being a Black woman with dyslexia and dyspraxia comes with many more exclusions. In 2022 I decided to be unapologetic about who I am and the changes that I want to see as a Black woman who is neurodiverse. Black people are still fighting to get a seat at the table in so many sectors, and I have noticed the same lack of inclusion in the world of neurodiversity. A lot of work is still needed, especially when it comes to inclusion, and it needs to be recognised that representation is key, and we need more people that look like us who can represent the greatness of dyslexia in every sector. If I can see it, I can be it, is a saying I absolutely love.

It's time to recognise that neurodiverse Black people need to be in every sector because of their greatness. They shouldn't be just invited as a tick-box inclusion exercise but because of their greatness and the impact their contribution can make. It's important for future generations to see progression so they can feel included and valued in any sector they choose to be in.

"Dyslexia is not just a difficulty, it's also a gift. I am so proud to have allies with dyslexia, doing

fantastic things and continuing despite their challenges to make positive contributions to their community and beyond. Big respect."

-Asher Hoyles, dyslexia author, fellow dyslexic

"Dyslexia is a huge part of my identity and without it I wouldn't be who I am today: a fearless, creative dance entrepreneur."

-Tamar, "Unique Tay," fellow dyslexic on a journey to empower dance and creative work

Empowering parents

"Dyslexia is not due to a lack of intelligence – it's a lack of access. It's like, if you're dyslexic, you have all the information you need, but find it harder to process." Orlando Bloom, Actor

I wish my own parents had known about dyslexia, as I didn't stand a chance of getting any support when I was a child because few people in Jamaica knew much about it. Even today, many still don't. I can imagine my parents talking about it. They would be saying, "Dys who?" "Dys what?" "A wha dat?"

Looking back, I remember how certain words like "dunce", "stupid", "idiat," "fool", and "jackass" would always get thrown around about us. Those words can follow us around for a lifetime, and today, they are still being used, which is a shame because none of those labels are true. There is still so much work to be done in Jamaica to raise awareness and help those children who are not getting any help or support.

I am excited and hopeful things are changing for the better in Jamaica, and more people are starting to get a better understanding of dyslexia. The Jamaica Dyslexia Association has been around for several years, helping to raise awareness. After seeing an article by the founder, Heather Christian, I reached out to her after we connected on LinkedIn, and she has been there encouraging and supporting me. Heather has a great story of her own experience of growing up in Jamaica as a dyslexic, and I am honoured she shared some of her own journey in my book. Heather is deeply passionate about helping others because, from her own experience, she knows what it feels like not having any support or knowing where to go for help. There is still a long way to go, but I am confident changes are coming as awareness increases. I love my home country and really want to help, and I would love to collaborate with an organisation on the same mission and do a school tour in Jamaica one day.

Travelling.

"My dyslexic thinking means I don't just think outside the box, I think outside the planet."

-Maggie Aderin-Pocock, space scientist, fellow dyslexic

Like many other dyslexics, I really struggle with travelling on the motorway, as the signs can be so confusing. My biggest challenge is listening to a satnav, reading the road signs and concentrating on the road all at the same time; doing all that is not easy when you are trying to get somewhere on time. Travelling to new cities can be difficult, with Birmingham being one of them, as the last time I went there, I was in tears. It was so frustrating as I spent over two hours driving around trying to find my prepaid parking, and, in the end, I had to give up and park somewhere else. On top of that, I got two tickets for driving in a clean-air zone. I had to appeal those charges because it was so difficult to even notice the signs while listening to the satnav and paying attention to the road.

Signage and Instructions.

I am sure it's not only me that has issues with signage, especially when driving. I wish it were simpler, as one of the hardest things is reading signs while driving. If it's raining, that's even worse, as it seems so confusing because you are driving and trying to remember what you just read and which junction is next while positioning on the road in the correct lane at the correct speed. Yes, it can all get very overwhelming. Manufacturers of signs and billboards should always think about people with learning differences, as we all see things differently.

Instructions can also be challenging for dyslexics, and it's important to break them down into little steps before starting and working out what needs to be done. I often get confused reading the instructions and then remembering what to do next. A good to follow instructions is to listen to then in a voice recording, instead of reading them, with the option of rewinding it, when you need to.

Websites.

The world of technology can be mind-boggling, to say the least, and for us dyslexics, it can become a battlefield. I commend the efforts of those that recognise the need to be inclusive and actually do something about it. Roger Broadbent has been a champion in helping companies and organisations make their websites dyslexic-friendly, and I am so grateful for the work he is doing to improve the online experience for those with Dyslexia.

Schools and the education system.

"There is no greater disability in society than the inability to see a person as more."

-Robert Hensel, disability activist

The school experience of a child will have a great impact on their future. I know the impact a good teacher can have on a child, whether positive or negative. I wish I could change so much of my schooling and the education system that wasn't made to understand me as an individual. My schooling in Jamaica had a great impact on the start of my education journey.

While I have many reasons to be resentful of the education system, I am still grateful for the work done globally to help change things for generations to come.

Teachers and lecturers should always recognise that we are all the same but different in our own way. Everyone does things differently, and each dyslexic will face different challenges. It can be even worse if they are teaching a student that hasn't been diagnosed and is struggling in silence. This is why I am so passionate about raising awareness of the importance of early diagnosis in school, to avoid the pain and struggles that can be felt without any support. I get frustrated when parents reach out to me because of the challenges they are having with their own children and the lack of support they are experiencing with their child's school. While writing this book, I was happy and excited to see that even government ministers were recognising the need for more support in schools and have called for early diagnosis to be a priority in schools.

Too Many Buttons.

"I want people to know that you can have dyslexia and still achieve your dreams."

-Darren Clark, dyslexia Influencer/award-winning entrepreneur/Neurodiversity Stories host/changing perceptions of neurodiversity globally through speaking, training and consulting, fellow dyslexic

While it was a childhood dream to be on the radio, I was terrified the first time I walked into the studios of BBC Radio Manchester. I remember looking at all the different buttons and dials, thinking about what they all did and why there were so many. It totally overwhelmed me all, and I was anxious looking at them.

While it was all overwhelming, it was also exciting because I knew I could do it, but I would need a lot of patience.

My Radio Diamond journey started when I appeared on Deanne Heron's show and then on Imani's show. These two ladies really encouraged me towards my dream of being on the radio. After starting on Radio Diamond, I was very anxious about learning what to do, but I was also eager to get started and learn and step into my dream of being a radio presenter. I always refer to myself as a presenter rather than a DJ, as I am not interested in being a DJ. I had a vision of using my voice on the radio to make a difference. When I created the Lady K Aspire to Inspire show, I knew I wanted to showcase inspiration, and interviewing others has become one of my greatest passions. I love giving others the opportunity to talk about themselves and what they are doing.

When I invite people for an interview, they often express their anxiety of being nervous and often ask whether I have a set of questions I can send them. My answer is always the same: I don't do scripted interviews, and it's just a chat. Being dyslexic, I like to keep things simple, and I pride myself on making the experience as enjoyable as possible, with no need for nervousness. After the interview, the feedback is always that I have great interview techniques, which made them feel at ease and relaxed. I do understand that sometimes it's their first time being interviewed on the radio, and I never want it to be an unpleasant experience but an enjoyable one.

I love hearing the inspirational stories of others in our communities that are striving to make a difference. It's something I am passionate about because I remember when I, too, didn't have a voice or the opportunity to be heard. I love networking and meeting great people, but it wasn't always like that. I was that shy, quiet girl, too and didn't want to speak up because I hated my voice from my experience of being bullied for the way I spoke and my accent. This is real evidence that when you stop believing in the limitations that others place on you, everything changes! What is yours can never be for someone else, so the opportunities that come your way are meant for you.

"It's really important to focus on the things you're good at, not the things you aren't. For me, it's out-of-the-box thinking and problem-solving, rather than spelling and grammar. Stay positive and believe in your abilities."

-Alison Edgar, MBE, chief SMASHER and managing director at SMASH IT! Training, communications expert and motivational speaker, fellow dyslexic

Ernst and Young Foundation

"The key to success is to tap into their own strengths and skills and be unafraid to think differently."

-Darren Clark, dyslexia Influencer/award-winning entrepreneur/Neurodiversity Stories host/changing perceptions of neurodiversity globally through speaking, training and consulting, fellow dyslexic

It's really exciting that Ernst & Young, the accountancy firm, has now opened a neurodiverse centre of excellence in Manchester, and another one will be opened in Glasgow in 2023, which will be hiring workers who have dyslexia, ADHD and autism. Ernst and Young have already created over fifteen neurodiverse centres of excellence globally.

This is a great development in recognition of the valuable thinking skills needed when developing technology. These centres will highlight the importance and benefits of having a neurodiverse workforce.

The Government

While writing this book, neurodiversity has been receiving more attention from businesses and the government. However, enough is still not being done to bring about more support for change. Matt Hancock, who was a government minister with dyslexia, has been campaigning for change, especially as the government is threatening to withdraw access to student loans for anyone unable to achieve their GCSE's. This change will significantly impact people with dyslexia, as many dyslexics leave school without achieving a single GCSE. I know – I was one of them. My determination led me to go on to achieve a first-class honours degree and then my master's. Not achieving GCSEs should not be a barrier to accessing funding for continued education.

Empowering
the dyslexic writer.

"I am a published author and have the freedom to use other sources like pictures and audio sounds and not rely totally on the written word." Natalie Teniola, author and founder of ICare Jamaica (fellow dyslexic)

I know you have a book in you, and not one, but many. For some, the thought of writing a book can seem so difficult or unachievable but take it from me; you can do it. It took me a while to finish my own book, but I didn't give up because here you are reading it now. The best advice I can give you is to get it out of your head and start writing things down. Just write. Take some time out to write and download the ideas into a plan you can work around. Schedule time each day to write. I know we all have some great ideas in our minds, but it's no use just being up there; get it out and down on paper bit by bit until you have your book. If all the other authors and I have done it, so can you.

A great way to get down what you want to say is to make use of assistive technology that can help to make the process less stressful and overwhelming. There are some great things you can use to help you, and each day, more and more technology is being developed to help with learning differences. It's important to work with people that understand you and the way you do things, so straight away, I knew that I had to publish my book with none other than the Author's Midwife, Marcia M. Spence. Marcia has worked with many other dyslexics I know in my network, and they received great support throughout the process. She is amazing at what she does, and I feel blessed to have her as part of my book journey. Remember that your book will serve as a legacy even when you are long gone. It's a great thing to inspire future generations and will be a constant reminder of your contribution to the world.

Motivation in Words

The ABC of encouragement

for dyslexics

A is for acceptance. Accept who you are and have a positive attitude towards being dyslexic!

B is for brilliant. Show off your brilliance everywhere you go and in all that you do! You are blessed!

C is for courageous. Be courageous in all your endeavours!

D is for dynamic. You are a dynamic individual with a different way of thinking!

E is for empowered. Feel it and believe that you are!

F is for fantastic because that is what you are. You have a very bright future ahead.

G is for gratitude. Be grateful for the blessing of being dyslexic or dyspraxic, as it is a gift!

H is for happiness. Be happy to be you with all you have been blessed with. You are highly favoured!

I is for intelligence. That is what you are: a highly intelligent and intellectual person with a great imagination!

J is for justification. Live with the belief you don't need to justify yourself to anyone!

K is for kindness. Others may not always be kind to you, but don't be like them. Kindness is something we all need in our lives

L is for love. No matter what, love yourself and look after yourself, as you are one in a million, and there is only one you!

M is for magnificent. You are all that and more! So never forget that!

N is for never giving up on your dreams and goals because you, too, can **achieve all you want!**

O is for original. You are one of a kind, and no one else can be you!

P is for purpose. Find your passion and connect it to your purpose; you are here for a reason and not by accident!

Q is for quiet. Never be quiet about who you are; don't be afraid to tell others that you are dyslexic or dyspraxic! Own it!

R is for respect. Have respect for yourself and for who you are. Remain true to yourself!

S is for strength. You have the strength to rise above any challenge you may face!

T is for thanks. Give thanks for your blessings and for being blessed with all that you have

U is for understanding. Many won't understand you, but understanding yourself is all that matters!

V is for victorious. You will have victory in all that you do and put your mind to!

W is for wonderful because that is what you are and always will be!

X is for the X factor. You are definitely the X factor, and don't let anybody tell you any different!

Y is for you. It's all about YOU. YOU have all it takes to do and be the best that you want to be.

Z is for zest. Keep your zest for life alive and keep on moving forward!

Hacks, tips and tricks for dyslexics.

It was an absolute honour to be part of the Dyslexia Life Hacks, which is a brilliant series by Matthew Head. I found these hacks immensely helpful, and I have included them in my book so that others can also benefit from using them in their everyday life. Thank you, Mathew, for creating such a great resource to help others.

Skill Swap

Keisha Swaby outlined this hack in episode seven of The Dyslexia Life Hacks Show.

Struggling to get something done? Sitting up late at night banging your head against the wall not helping? Then skill swap with your friend who is awesome at it (they can also help patch you up after you've hit your head against the wall).

We all have strengths and challenges, and no one person is brilliant at everything. Swapping a skill is a powerful way of getting the task done on time and learning new skills from your friends and colleagues, in time teaching them new things too!

They can help teach that skill you are struggling with, and in return, you can help with a skill they're having bother with. It is a great way of building strong relationships, social connections, and camaraderie.

Timing with tomatoes to boost productivity

Find yourself getting really distracted when you need to get a task done, whether it's wanting to check Facebook or look at that email that just came in? Then you can use the Pomodoro Technique, named after a Pomodoro kitchen timer and described by Ian in Episode 21 of The Dyslexia Life Hacks Show.

This great technique uses short intervals of time with small breaks that help you: 1) get into a task you are struggling with: and 2) get some good quality work/studying with full focus. Then in the breaks, you can indulge in social media or whatever takes your fancy. It also gives you a break from the screen.

How to use the technique:

1. Eliminate all distractions (yes, that does mean putting your phone on silent)

2. Set a timer for 25 minutes

3. Work on your task

4. When the timer is finished, take a 5-minute break

5. Get back to work for another 25 minutes

6. After 4 work sessions, take a longer break of 25 minutes

7. Start all over again

Use this as a start and adjust the timings to suit you.

You can either buy a Pomodoro kitchen timer or a stopwatch, and there are lots of apps out there that you can use.

Be Bold and Think Differently

Trevor sent this hack. He was the first person to send a hack in. Thank you, Trevor!

In school, specifically in English class, pupils would be asked to read aloud. This was usually from books or short stories. When it came to dyslexic pupils, they would stumble through words, often having to reread an entire sentence to fluently say it. The teacher would say, "It's your turn to read pages 56 through 58," filling them with dread. Then, one day, when asked to read, they said, "Pass." The class looks around, thinking, 'You can do that! You can just pass on reading?' To everyone's surprise, it worked! The teacher was confused and didn't know how to respond because no one had ever challenged it. They said "okay" and moved to the next person.

The moral of the story is to be bold and think differently. Just because it's been done the same way forever doesn't mean it has to be done that way.

Self-limiting beliefs are ideas you hold on to that you believe are facts. These can range from anything such as, 'I'm too old to take up that sport' to 'I can't handle conflict'. In reality, these beliefs are holding you back from taking up that sport or resulting in you giving in to others.

Some of my self-limiting beliefs when it comes to dyslexia were:

- I can't go to university – that's what smart people do.

- I will never be able to learn properly.

- Being dyslexic only has a downside.

Once, nobody thought a mile could be run in less than four minutes. Once this belief had been shattered, lots of people started doing it.

The same is true when it comes to dyslexia. Dyslexic individuals are smart and, of course, also go to university and get top-quality degrees. Dyslexic individuals are exceptionally good at mastery and can learn new skills well. Most importantly, having dyslexia is also a gift and brings many positive things to you and the world.

So, when you hear that voice in your head saying you can't do it, tell it you're going to prove it wrong.

You've Got a Friend in Me!

The best and most important hack of them all: surround yourself with great friends that you care about and care about you. Your friends are great for proofreading that application you are about to make or the website you have built (like the number of my friends who proofread this one). Not only a proof-reader, but you can also have some fun times laughing and making humour of your dyslexic works. They're a good sounding board for understanding the issues non-dyslexics have with things and highlighting your positive traits.

Do Not Hit That Send Button

The send button is there, tempting you to hit it the moment you finish an email or text message. It can be the misheld belief of some dyslexics – and until recently one held by me – that 'normal' people can write a text message or email and do not have to go back to edit it. This is not right – having spoken to plenty of people on this, I know they always wait five to ten minutes before sending their emails as they need to proofread them and sometimes realise the initial message made no sense at all. If you, like me, have held this belief for years, it may come as a massive surprise. It is a good habit to cultivate. If you have time, pause before sending, particularly emails and text messages (although most of my friends now understand my unique take on the English language!).

Record a Presentation and Then Write It Down

Presentation to deliver at work or a best man speech. Did you struggle to write the speech out by hand and then learn it traditionally? Then don't. Think about your speech while driving the car, having a shower, or riding a motorbike. Talking aloud will give you a feel for how it will sound to your audience. Then use the audio notes app on your phone to record some initial ideas. Start making bullet points – you will be surprised how the speech starts to fall out of you, and you can use the bullet points as prompts to refine your speech. This is how I approach my speechwriting now. Maybe a few notes here and there, then work through it in my head, speaking out loud and refining it from there.

Be Good to Yourself

"Sometimes the only positive things you will hear about yourself are what you tell yourself, so be good to yourself and always speak positively about yourself."

-Valerie Campbell, motivational speaker, fellow dyslexic

As dyslexics, we can be extremely critical about ourselves and our work and very hard on ourselves due to the fear of being criticised, that we are not good enough or just plain old imposter syndrome. We have endured names like dumb and lazy along the way due to ignorance and lack of understanding. Whoopi Goldberg is a prime example of how acceptance can help you understand how amazing you can be when you realise your true potential.

Not believing in yourself is often a result of low self-esteem and lack of confidence. It's important to understand that it's down to you. No one can be you. You are good enough to do and achieve anything you want. No matter what challenges you are faced with, you can achieve anything.

Learn to accept who you are and that you are highly intelligent with extraordinary skills that are needed in all areas of society. For example, it has been said that more companies and organisations are recognising dyslexic strengths, and it has been reported that 50 per cent of

NASA's employees are dyslexic. This is great proof that dyslexics are in high demand for their skills. Don't sweat the small stuff, as we are great at finding solutions to problems in any situation and have a lot of empathy, always trying to help others. Comparing yourself with others can lead to feelings of failure because you think things are not happening for you but are happening for others. Be inspired by others, but don't compare yourself with them. If you admire or are inspired by something someone else is doing, connect with them and ask for advice. You can't be them, and they can't be you, so think collaboration, not competition.

"I love me so that I can love you. Self-sabotage is what people do when they have dyslexia. But once they choose to accept their gift, self-love comes, and they flourish like a flower. So now I love me so that I can love you."

-Karlet Manning, mental health practitioner, fellow dyslexic.

Don't be ashamed.

"My experience with dyslexia as a young person was like being trapped in a dark room on my own, struggling to navigate. However, once I became aware of my condition, and owned it, the lights went on. I could see clearly, as I knew what was happening. I was able to share my story with others who were also struggling. We see especially those from BAME communities who don't have the confidence to share their stories and be heard. I encourage everyone to be bold, speak up, own the experience. Dyslexia is not something to be ashamed of. It's just part of the human experience."

-Martin Daay, founder of Project Daaylight, fellow dyslexic

Being dyslexic, I have always found it easy to spot mistakes in other people's work but not in my own. I know the mistakes I make, so it's easy for me to spot them.

I want to shout from the rooftops that dyslexia is nothing to be ashamed of. In the Black community, many myths exist about dyslexia. For example, many think it's a curse rather than a blessing with many positive attributes to offer to the world. Be proud of the skills you have been gifted with.

As I continue to make my dreams come true!

"Each successful dyslexic has a chip on their shoulder to prove everyone who ever doubted their ability wrong, to prove that they are not stupid or thick."

-Neil Alexander-Passe

The dreams that I have held in my heart growing up are finally coming true. I have always wanted to work in the media with a keen interest in radio and television. I love creativity, and I am so happy to be living out these dreams, and to date, I have appeared on several tv shows aired on BBC1, SKY and Channel 4. I am grateful to be part of an amazing agency that is helping me to fulfil these dreams. Thank you for all the support you give me and the opportunities I now get to work with amazing production teams, and actors.

What next?

I have a deep desire to help make a change and bring more awareness to dyslexia and dyspraxia globally. Having children who are also neurodiverse makes it a personal mission, as I want things to be better not just for them but also for generations to come. I have dedicated plenty of time and effort to highlighting the strengths of being dyslexic and that it's okay to think and do things differently. Whilst the work I do is not to collect accolades, it was encouraging to be recognised as one of the top 50 most influential neurodivergent women by Beyond the Box. It was an absolute honour to be a finalist for Role model of the Year at the MBCC awards and to receive an award for community unsung hero from the Caribbean, African Health Network (CAHN). Grateful to everyone who nominated and voted for me. Whilst I am not sure who nominated me for the Northern Power Women 2023 future list, thank you to whoever it is.

Earlier this year, I was invited to be part of an exciting project with Ayoa, and I had the privilege of working with Ross and Morgan. It was such a great experience, and I just want to say to them both for the inclusion and for the hospitality when I visited their office. Thank you to everyone involved.

Sharing our lived experiences help others to understand us more, and I want to do more inspirational talks in schools, colleges, universities, and in the workplace, so if you are reading this and need a speaker, don't hesitate to reach out for a chat to see how we can work together.

'Blessed & Gifted'

Be empowered!

"A message to my dyslexic brothers and sisters:

"Be brave to dream big and reach out for your goals, but at the same time take care of your whole self – build healthy habits: eat well, exercise, develop strong relationships with neighbours, family, and friends.

"Find your skills and improve them, and work on the areas you might need to enhance.

"You are brilliant. Respect yourself and those around you, and let's see what you can achieve!" Roger Broadbent, director,

-Dyslexia Institute UK, fellow dyslexic

Don't ever forget you are truly blessed and gifted! Don't place any limits on your abilities, as you are limitless, with great potential.

It would be a very dull world if we were all the same. Embrace who you are and what you have been sent here to accomplish! What you think of yourself is all that matters; what others think of you is none of their business, as everyone has their own life to live!

You are good enough, so don't ever compare your abilities and your achievement with others, as we all learn and do things differently! No one can ever be you because you are the original, not the copy! It all starts with you, so believe in yourself and your abilities in everything you do!

You will have days when you feel down and frustrated, but continue to trust the process, and it will all be fine!

Do things that make you feel happy and excited. Do the things that make your heart sing! Embrace your gifts and superpowers as you have been given them for a reason. Don't ever be ashamed that you may be dyslexic. The more you embrace it, the more you will feel empowered and be able to get the support you need and be the success for which you were created.

Your light is bright, so let it shine. You deserve to walk in your purpose, so keep going no matter what! Fall in love with your uniqueness and pay attention to your strengths. Don't focus on your challenges.

Our Superpower!!

I can confidently say God has blessed me with a gift, and I am proud of who I am and all the purpose I was made for. I will be forever grateful for my superpower; I own it, and I am proud of it.

Go out there and pursue your dreams and let nothing stop you. Your talents are limitless, and you are extraordinary. Determination will take you a long way, and you have the drive to achieve all that you put your mind to.

Go out there and show the world that you are not ordinary; you are extraordinary in many ways.

Never forget how amazing you are and how blessed you are to be you; everyone is uniquely created, and you are here to make a difference.

You have been created for greatness. believe that you can make it, one step and one day at a time. Remember that there is a neurodiverse community here to cheer you on.

You are not alone.

Keisha Adair Swaby

Just want to say thank you ...

There are some awesome people that I have met over the years, many through the power of social media. I have received some great help and support from my connections, whom I have met at events on Facebook, LinkedIn and Instagram. The dyslexic community on LinkedIn is amazing, and it's always great to connect with anyone with a link to neurodiversity.

Believe me when I say there are plenty of us. I have to say LinkedIn has been a blessing as I have met some amazing, supportive people on that platform. I have received continuous support and encouragement from many, near and far.

Some significant people have helped me on this journey, and I really appreciate you all.

Big thanks and appreciation to the following:-

Eric

My friend of more than twenty-seven years, you have always been there encouraging me. Throughout my studies, you held me accountable to ensure that I was putting in the work to meet my assignment deadlines.

When I felt like giving up and didn't believe I would ever finish writing this book, your encouragement helped me push through and see the bigger picture. You are a true friend who is not afraid of telling me off when I was not writing enough and needed to be told. While you have never been formally diagnosed, I often see the superpower traits you possess in the way you do things.

You are brilliant at finding solutions and have a great understanding of people and a heart full of empathy for others. I thank you for being on my case to get my book completed. Continue being the great person that you are. I appreciate you even when you give me the biggest telling-off and cussing, but I know you always mean well as one friend to another, and it did work because here is the book. Thank you for seeing my dream and believing in me and my abilities. I really and truly appreciate your patience and persistence on my journey to becoming an author. Thanks, and appreciation to you always.

Dr Louise Harvey-Golding

I am incredibly grateful to you, the lady who helped me realise I had it in me to start my university journey. Thank you for seeing what I didn't see and for your belief and inspiration. Now you have a Doctorate, I applaud you for your persistence in going after your own dream and being an inspiration to people like me. If I hadn't left my job, where we met, I would never have known I had dyslexia. Continue to shine and inspire us women to go after it, whatever it may be. Thank you!

Dr Ava Eagle Brown

Thank you for your inspiration as my book journey started with you. I truly admire your determination and resilience to carry on no matter what. Your saying of your book is your hook has always stayed with me. Keep on being the inspiration that you truly are.

Jean Campbell

My other mother, you have been there, and I want to thank you for keeping your promise to my grandma to always look out for me.

Samantha Douglas-Johnson

Sam, thank you for being there and for your continuous support over the years. Thank you for the fun and laughter we have had. You are always there for my ups and downs with a listening ear and supportive shoulder. Growing up together, we have shared so many fun times. Love and appreciation to you always.

Candice Douglas

My little cousin, I am so proud of you and the very inspirational young lady that you have become. Continue to shine your light and inspire your children to be the best they can be. Thank you.

Abigail Etim-Reid

Abigail, thank you for your continued support on my journey, for your contribution to the creative industry, and for your passion for educating others about our beautiful Jamaica through your story sessions, which my son has had the opportunity to be part of.

Nicola Cartwright

We have been blessed as a family to have you in our lives. You have done so much for my family and me over the years. I want you to know I appreciate you. You are my true sister and I have so much love for you and your family. While we may not see each other often, you know I am here, and you are there whenever I need you.

Helen Kent-Jackson

My amazing mentor. From the Lloyds Banking Group. I have so many ideas and they helped me to focus on what needs to be done and how to prioritise things.

Shaletta B. Perry

My American Sister, in 2019, you invited us to Atlanta, and we had the opportunity to attend your royal event from princess to a queen. It was my first time travelling to America and it is an experience that I always think about.

Kemi Olunde Obisesan

Ever since we met, you have been one of my biggest cheerleaders in all that I do. We have shared some great memories on our trip to Atlanta and all the jokes we shared are still fresh in my memory.

Charity Tembo Pepuzani

I only have to answer the phone, and it's pure laughter between us. The things we reminisce about never fail to make us burst out in fits of laughter. Thank you for the great memories that we created on our trip to Atlanta.

Heather Christian

My Jamaican dyslexic mother. This lady is so special to me. While we have never met in person, you have influenced my life and have been there since we met online. Thank you for your amazing support and for giving me the opportunity to be an Ambassador of the Jamaica

Dyslexic Association. You inspire me so much. It is an absolute honour to include part of your story in my book.

Maserat Parveen

Maz, I have so much to thank you for, especially your friendship. You have encouraged me from day one, and it was a blessing meeting you in 2016.

UCEN Manchester

Thank you for playing such a significant part in my journey. I thoroughly enjoyed my time studying with you and for all the great support I received from all the lecturers and the student support team.

Lesley French

Lesley French, I owe so much to you all. I will never forget the day your discovery changed everything for me. You gave me so much support and encouragement and the great laughs we had in the library. If it wasn't for you checking my work, I still wouldn't have known I had dyslexia and dyspraxia. I will be forever grateful for the impact you have had on my life. Meeting you on my journey has contributed to all the great things I am doing to help others.

Manchester Metropolitan University

I knew I would get to study there one day and walking through that door on the Birley Fields campus was a long-awaited part of my journey. In 2019 I attended the first lecture of my master's in health psychology; I can remember the day very well, especially having to go up and down those stairs in the middle of that building. I was so scared of tripping up and I had to always make sure I was holding on to the side rail to stop me from missing my step. I have to commend the disability support services for the support I received from all the staff during my master's. I really felt supported, and I made a great choice to study at MMU.

Dr Melissa Pilkington

> *"No significant learning occurs without a significant relationship."*
>
> *-Dr James P. Comer, Yale Child Study Center*

As my personal tutor in the first year of my master's at Manchester Metropolitan University, I am grateful for your help and support. The fact you are another successful dyslexic made me feel at ease because you understand me. Understanding and relatability are so important. Teachers and lecturers can play an incredibly significant role in the success of their students. This is why it is so important that their learning styles are known to provide the right support.

Students with dyslexia can excel in the right environment, especially one that understands and supports their learning style. I felt understood, which helped my confidence in knowing there was someone I could talk to about the challenges I was facing. For example, you understood without judgement when I mistyped and put my letters in the wrong places. When you have someone in your corner who understands why you do things and the way you do them, it makes a big difference. It was great to work with Melissa on my dissertation because no matter how frustrated I was about the amount of work I had completed since our last meeting, she made me feel at ease and reassured me I was doing great. While reminding me not to be too hard on myself. Mel would always encourage me to take time out for myself and look after 'me' while working on my dissertation. I will be forever grateful for her help and understanding.

Jacqui Flisher

I will be forever grateful for your support and guidance. I am blessed to have met you and I genuinely appreciate your guidance and support in all I do. Whenever I need you for a chat or advice, you always find the time for me. I remember when I asked you to be my mentor, and without hesitation, you said yes. I am honoured to have you in my life and grateful for all I can learn from you as my mentor.

Pamela R Haynes

I have watched your journey from the start and have been inspired by your determination with your own book. Having you in our network has been a blessing in so many ways. One of the greatest things you have done for me is to connect me to Marcia Brissett Bailey

Marcia Brissett-Bailey

My Dyslexic soul sister has been there for me throughout this journey. We connected through Pamela R Haynes, and I am so grateful that she introduced us. You have been a rock and I thank you for all your help in running the Empowering Dyslexics Facebook Group and for our sister chats. Thank you for writing the foreword for my book and for all your continued support.

Zoe-Jane Littlewood

Zoe, I am so inspired by your determination and willingness to help others. I am blessed to have met you.

Marcia M. Publishing House

Marcia M Publishing House Team for their collective contributions to the editing, reading, design, promotion and distribution of *Empowering Dyslexics*.

A massive thank you to all the great people listed below who have contributed in some way to my life and my endeavours.

Everyone at Radio Diamond

All my siblings in Jamaica, Letty, Pat, Shane and Akeil, my Nieces and Nephews, along with all my other family and friends in Jamaica, England, Barbados, America, Canada.

Adam Howard

Adeyinka Adewumi

Akua Opong

Alex Onalaja

Andrew Kitley

Angie Le Mar

Arran Smith

Auntie Girtie

Benjamin James Kershaw

Beverly Joye Smith

Brenda Campbell

Carol Ann Whitehead

Carol Stewart

Charles Kwaku-Odoi

Christina Luke

Christine Giscombe

Colin Redman

David C Hall

Dawn Campbell

Deborah Leveroy

Denise Douglas – Armstrong

Denise Harvey

Dexter Mcintosh

Dimar Creatives

Dionne Samuels

Dollie Wright

Donla Campbell

Dr Faye Bruce

Dr Tru Powell

EJ

Ekua Cant

Elayne Harriott

Elizabeth Cameron

Elizabeth Takyi

Emma Case

Errol Douglas

Fiona Gray

Gary Thomas

Hakim Smith

Helen Heap

Imani Speaks

Jack Churchill

Jannett Morgan

Jannette Barrett

Jay Blades MBE

Jessica Kennedy Falconer

Jessica Taylor

Jerdine Baker

Joanna Grzesiak

Joanne Swaby

Joe Guant

Jon Talarico

Josephine Perruzza

Julianna Mango

Julie Mango

Kaydia Edwards

Karen Cruise

Karen Openshaw

Karla Marie

Karlene Agard

Kemoy Walker

Kerissa Nelson

Kerome Layor

Kerry Mellor

Khori Hyde

Knowledge

Krystle Mcgilvery

Lakisha Grant

Larry Wright

Lee Chambers

Les Brown

Lesleye O'Connor

LeTeisha Wright

Linda Ernest

Lois Letchford

Marcia M. Spence

Maisie Barrett

Mark Dodd

Mark Potts

Mark Swaby

Martin Bloomfield

Melissa Desveaux

Merline Ulysse

Mica Virova

Monica Ledgister

Monique Pink

Naomi Brown

Naomi Forrest Hamilton

Natalie Carr

Nathan Beattie

Nathan Dodd

Nathaniel Peat

Odaine Mills

Onyinye Udokporo

Paloma Forde

Pamela Aculey Kosminsky

Paul Carrick Brunson

Paul Morrison

Paulette Simpson CBE

Pele Hunkin

Rachael Harper

Rachel Hawkins

Radika Drummond Campbell

Rebecca Henderson

Rebecca Hollyoak

Rebecca Solomon-Henry

Roger Broadbent

Rohan Baker (Buckles)

Sanchia Alasia

Sandra Brown

Sandra Trew

Shah Siddiqui

Sharlene Small

Sharon Amesu

Sharon Dawn Linton - Faulkner

Shaun Pascal

Sherrie Rose Hamilton

Shirley May

Simone Riley

Sonia Poleon

Stuart Marsden

Suzanne Hall

Tarnya Coley

Tasharnae Douglas

Theo Dell

Tomarley Dodd

Toni Hall

Tori Roberts

Tracy Roachford

Valerie Campbell

Vanessa Peat

Waldine Howard

Will Wheeler

Yanique Taylor

Yashica Broughton

Yvonne Dodd

Yvonne Johnson

Zara Aflick

Resources for Dyslexics

Films Highlighting Dyslexia

Night School, starring Kevin Hart
Mical
The Big Picture: Rethinking Dyslexia
Journey into Dyslexia
Like Stars on Earth
Dislecksia: The Movie
Inside Dyslexia
The Secret
Embracing Dyslexia
Read me Differently
Being You

Technology to Help Dyslexics

Claro Software
Sanocent
Scanning Pens
Dragon Naturally Speaking
TextHelp
Read&Write

References

Association, B. (2019) About dyslexia - British Dyslexia Association. British Dyslexia Association. [Online] [Accessed on 1 July 2019] https://www.bdadyslexia.org.uk/dyslexia/about-dyslexia.

Kaplan, B., N. Wilson, B., Dewey, D. and Crawford, S. (1998). DCD may not be a discrete disorder. Human Movement Science, 17(4-5), pp.471-490.

Schools 'failing to diagnose at least 80% of dyslexic pupils'. (2021) BBC News. [Online] [Accessed on 19 June 2021] https://www.bbc.co.uk/news/uk-england-50095218.

Robinson, J. (2019) 'BECKHAM'S BATTLE: Victoria Beckham claims she's a "self-diagnosed dyslexic" and says her children also struggle with it'. [online] *The Sun*. [Accessed on 9 November 2021]

Useful websites

https://www.bdadyslexia.org.uk/dyslexia

https://www.thesun.co.uk/tvandshowbiz/8651196/victoria-beckham-self-diagnosed-dyslexic-children-struggle/.

https://www.change.org/p/isle-of-man-to-sign-the-made-by-dyslexia-pledge-and-follow-gibraltar-s-lead?utm_source=share_petition&utm_medium=custom_url&recruited_by_id=338bdfc0-17ac-11ea-bc60-a37af053e039&use_react=false

https://www.bbc.co.uk/news/uk-50206103

Celebrating Successful Black Dyslexics/Dyspraxics
https://youtu.be/nyrSVW3Mri8

www.marciampublishing.com

Printed in Great Britain
by Amazon

20491286R00119